Math Dictionary
for Young People

Eula Ewing Monroe

Professor of Mathematics Education,
Brigham Young University
Professor Emeritus, Western Kentucky University

Silver Burdett Press • Parsippany, New Jersey

My deepest appreciation:

To Robert Panchyshyn of Western Kentucky University, a valued colleague and lifetime friend—for his leadership in analyzing terminology needed to learn mathematics and for his inspiration and encouragement for further study.

To Wilburn Jones, also of Western Kentucky University, my mentor in mathematics content—for his review of the manuscript for accuracy and approriateness for developing mathematicians.

To the administration of the BYU School of Education and to my colleagues in the Department of Teacher Education—for their enthusiastic support of my professional endeavors.

To the editors at Silver Burdett Press—for their guidance throughout this project.

To Bobbi, Becky, Chris, Danae, Jessica, Julie, Megan, Melissa, and Michelle—for the many hours they devoted to the details of my work.

To Matt, Jamie, and Roger—for loving me unconditionally.

To Kathy, the pastor, and other members of First Baptist Church of Provo and to D'Lynn—for their continuing support and prayers.

To my Lord and Savior—for the sure knowledge that this work has been within His plan for my life and that all things are possible through Him.

Library of Congress Cataloging-in-Publications
Monroe, Eula Ewing.
  Math dictionary for young people/by Eula Ewing Monroe.
       p. cm.
  Summary: A mathematics dictionary containing core words
  and related terms representing central math ideas.
  ISBN 0-382-39630-8. — ISBN 0-382-39631-6 (pbk.)
  1. Mathematics — Dictionaries, Juvenile. [1. Mathematics—Dictionaries.] I. Title
  QA5.M58 1998
  510'.3—dc21   97-1069
                       CIP
                       AC

Cover: Design—Ruth Otey
       Production—Robert Dobaczewski

Illustrations: pages 8, 31, 37, 50, 59, 61, 66, 67, 82, 83, 91, 100, 108, 112, 129, 139, ©1998 Bernard Adnet

Published by Silver Burdett Press
A Division of Simon & Schuster
299 Jefferson Road
Parsippany, NJ 07054-0480

First Edition
Printed in the United States of America
10 9 8 7 6 5 4 3 2 1

Contents

Message to Teachers and Parents

What Is In This Dictionary?

The *Math Dictionary for Young People* includes definitions for more than 600 terms needed in the study of mathematics, Grades 4–6. The language is user-friendly and mathematically appropriate for these grade levels. Whenever possible, everyday language has been used in definitions and examples; when technical language was needed for accurate communication of a mathematical concept, it was derived from vocabulary introduced at earlier grade levels. Examples, diagrams, pictures, and interesting facts are included to make definitions more explicit and to provide bridges to other mathematical ideas and to the real world.

The entries in this dictionary were selected based on extensive study of the terms included in textbooks and other mathematics materials used by students in grades 4–6. Most of the terms are considered core, or basic, vocabulary needed for the study of mathematics at these grade levels (for example, **fraction**). A few lesser-known terms (for example, **googol**) are included because they represent interesting mathematical ideas.

This dictionary, though designed primarily for children, should also be helpful to classroom teachers, parents, and others who want to understand the language of mathematics.

Why Learn the Language of Mathematics?

Benjamin Whorf, a noted linguist, hypothesized that language is necessary for higher-level thinking; moreover, an individual's language structure and development shape his or her understanding of the world (Carroll, 1956). Lev Semenovich Vygotsky, a Russian cognitive psychologist, theorized that the intellectual development of children is dramatically affected by their interaction with language (Vygotsky, 1962, 1978, cited in Reutzel & Cooter, 1996). The work of these and other scholars who have studied relationships between language and thought supports the current emphasis on communication in the learning of mathematics.

In 1989 the National Council of Teachers of Mathematics (NCTM) published a landmark document entitled *Curriculum and Evaluation Standards for School Mathematics*, followed by *Professional Standards for Teaching Mathematics* (1991) and *Assessment Standards for School Mathematics* (1995). These documents articulate a near consensus among the mathematics education community regarding the need for rich and meaningful communication in the teaching and learning of mathematics. The ability to communicate mathematically is viewed as a central goal for each learner, to be addressed in all aspects of mathematics instruction and assessment.

Guide to the Use of the Dictionary

Entry Words are highlighted in blue and have been carefully selected for their usefulness in learning mathematics. When entry words are continued on a subsequent page, this is indicated by the word *(continued)*.

Did You Know? relates interesting facts or ideas about the adjoining entry word.

Thumb Index Letters indicate the letter of the alphabet that the entry words on the page begin with. They appear at the top, middle, or bottom of the outside margin, depending upon their order in the alphabet.

Photographs and Illustrations have been selected to show real-world connections for many mathematical terms.

Guide Words at the top of each spread indicate the first and last entry word to appear on that spread.

AM—approximate number

AM

AM is used to label the time between midnight and noon. Also written as A.M., am, and a.m.

Did You Know?

A.M. is the abbreviation for *ante meridiem*, a Latin phrase meaning " before noon."

A

angle

An angle is formed when two line segments or rays meet at a common point.

An angle is described by the amount of turn from one ray or line segment to another. The amount of turn is measured in degrees (°).

ray   A ray is a part of a line that has one endpoint and extends infinitely in one direction.

right angle A right angle has a " square corner." Its measure is 90°.

acute angle An acute angle has a measure of less than 90°.

obtuse angle An obtuse angle has a measure of more than 90° but less than 180°.

straight angle A straight angle has a measure of two right angles, or 180°.

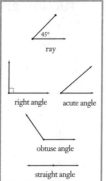

45°

ray

right angle   acute angle

obtuse angle

straight angle

12

Related Terms are often included under entry words in order to provided added or explanatory information. The related terms appear in blue.

Diagrams are used to illustrate mathematical concepts.

Related Words are mathematical terms whose root word is the entry word

Tools of the Trade illustrates those tools used to perform mathematical operations. These tools are also used by professionals in jobs such as design and architecture.

See Also links the entry words to synonyms, similar terms, or other terms in the dictionary that may extend understanding.

Definitions for each entry word are user-friendly for both students and their teachers. Related terms are included where appropriate.

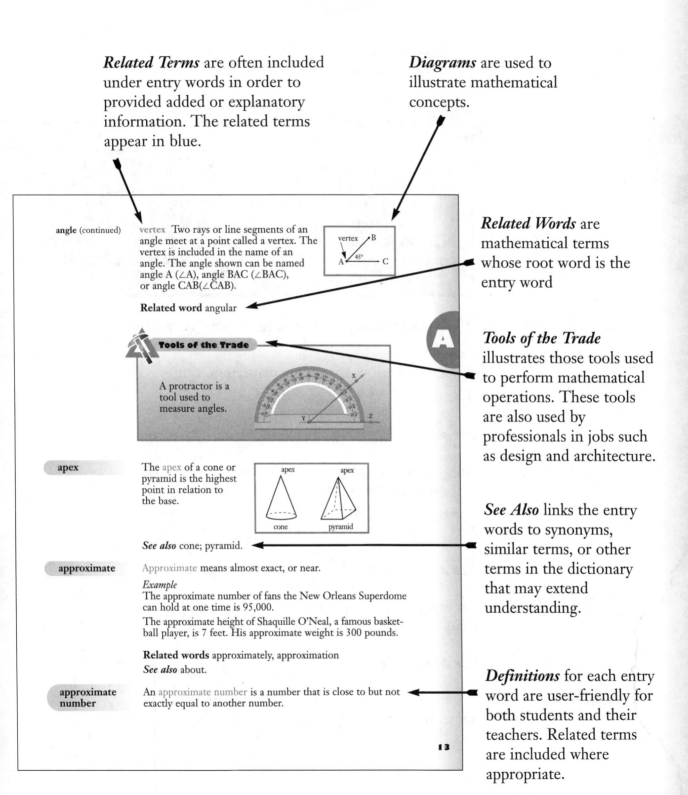

angle (continued)

vertex Two rays or line segments of an angle meet at a point called a vertex. The vertex is included in the name of an angle. The angle shown can be named angle A (∠A), angle BAC (∠BAC), or angle CAB(∠CAB).

Related word angular

Tools of the Trade

A protractor is a tool used to measure angles.

apex

The apex of a cone or pyramid is the highest point in relation to the base.

cone   pyramid

See also cone; pyramid.

approximate

Approximate means almost exact, or near.

Example
The approximate number of fans the New Orleans Superdome can hold at one time is 95,000.

The approximate height of Shaquille O'Neal, a famous basketball player, is 7 feet. His approximate weight is 300 pounds.

Related words approximately, approximation
See also about.

approximate number

An approximate number is a number that is close to but not exactly equal to another number.

abacus

pl. **abaci** An abacus is a device used for counting or doing operations.

Tools of the Trade

The abacus is an ancient device that is still used in China and Japan. In the U.S. it is often used to help demonstrate the concept of place value.

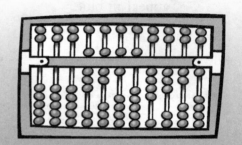

about

About means "almost the same as" or "very close to."

Examples
A stick of gum is about 7 centimeters long.
The sum of $2\frac{1}{2}$ and $\frac{1}{4}$ is about 3.

See also approximate.

acre

An acre is a unit for measuring area in the customary system of measurement.
1 acre = 43,560 ft²
640 acres = 1 mi²

See also customary system of measurement.

acute angle

An acute angle is an angle that measures less than 90°.

See also angle.

acute angle

acute triangle

An acute triangle is a triangle with three acute angles, which are angles measuring less than 90°.

See also triangle.

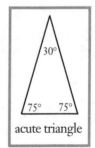

acute triangle

addend	An addend is a number that is to be added to another number.
	Examples
	In $3 + 6 = 9$, In $1.34 + 7\frac{1}{4} = 8.59$,
	3 and 6 are addends. 1.34 and $7\frac{1}{4}$ are addends.
	See also addition.
addition	Addition is a way of finding the number of two sets or quantities that are put together. It is an arithmetic operation. (The four basic arithmetic operations are addition, subtraction, multiplication, and division.)
	Related words add, addend, additive, additional
	See also addition fact; addition sentence.
addition facts	The basic addition facts are the 100 addition combinations of one-digit numbers.
	Examples
	$5 + 0 = 5$ $8 + 6 = 14$
	See also basic facts.
addition sentence	An addition sentence is a number sentence used to express addition.
	Example
	$10.3 + 7.2 = 17.5$
	In $10.3 + 7.2 = 17.5$,
	10.3 and 7.2 are addends.
	+ is the symbol for addition.
	17.5 is the sum.
	See also addend; addition; number sentence; sum.
addition table	The addition table is a table that shows the 100 basic addition facts.
	See also basic facts.
additive inverse	The additive inverse of a number is a number that is the same distance from 0 on the number line, but in the opposite direction. Also called opposite of a number.

A

A

additive inverse
(continued)

Example
$^+3 + {}^-3 = 0$
In the example, $^+3$ and $^-3$ are additive inverses, or opposites.

$^-3$ is the additive inverse, or opposite, of $^+3$.
$^+3$ is the additive inverse, or opposite, of $^-3$.

See also additive inverse property; opposite of a number.

additive inverse property

The additive inverse property is that the sum of a number and its opposite is 0. Also called inverse property of addition.

algebra

Algebra is a branch of mathematics in which arithmetic is extended to deal with unknown numbers or relationships, using letters or other symbols.

variable Symbols used to represent unknown numbers or relationships are called variables.

Example
Tyler counted the empty spaces in his stamp book.
He found that he needs to collect only 37 more stamps to fill his book, which holds 500 stamps.
How many stamps does he have already?

To solve this problem using algebra, first write an equation that describes the problem situation.

$s + 37 = 500$
Let s represent the number of stamps that Tyler already has. One way to solve for s is to subtract 37 from each side of the equation.

$s + 37 - 37 = 500 - 37$
$s = 463$
Tyler already has 463 stamps.

Related word algebraic
See also variable.

algorithm

An algorithm is a systematic step-by-step procedure.

partial products The following procedure is an algorithm for algorithm multiplication. It is often used for paper-and-pencil multiplication of numbers with two or more digits. (It is called the partial products algorithm.)

algorithm
(continued)

Example

```
  24
× 13   Step 1: Think of 13 as 10 + 3.
  72   Step 2: 3 × 24 = 72
 240   Step 3: 10 × 24 = 240
 312   Step 4: 72 + 240 = 312
```

Related word algorithmic

altitude

An altitude of a geometric figure is a line segment that shows the figure's height. Altitude is also the length of that line segment. Also called height. Altitude can also be used to mean elevation, or distance above sea level.

Examples
The altitudes for the following geometric figures are perpendicular to both bases. The altitude of the cylinder is line segment AB, or 1.5 centimeters.

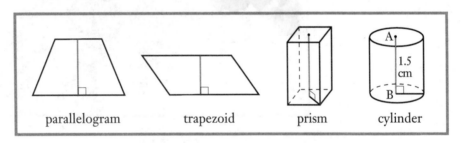

parallelogram   trapezoid   prism   cylinder

For a pyramid or cone, the altitude is a line segment from the vertex perpendicular to the base.

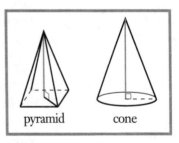

pyramid   cone

A triangle has three altitudes because any one of its sides can be a base. Notice that for some triangles, altitudes may be drawn both inside and outside the triangle.

See also height.

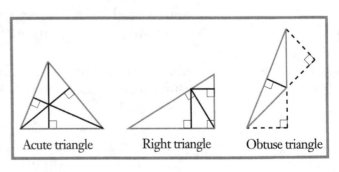

Acute triangle   Right triangle   Obtuse triangle

AM

AM is used to label the time between midnight and noon. Also written as A.M., am, and a.m.

Did You Know?

A.M. is the abbreviation for *ante meridiem*, a Latin phrase meaning "before noon."

A

angle

An angle is formed when two line segments or rays meet at a common endpoint.

An angle is described by the amount of turn around an endpoint from one ray or line segment to another. The amount of turn is measured in degrees (°).

ray A ray is a part of a line that has one endpoint and extends infinitely in one direction.

right angle A right angle has a "square corner." Its measure is 90°.

acute angle An acute angle has a measure of less than 90°.

obtuse angle An obtuse angle has a measure of more than 90° but less than 180°.

straight angle A straight angle has a measure of two right angles, or 180°.

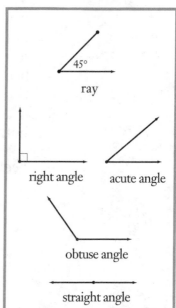

angle (continued)

vertex Two rays or line segments of an angle meet at a point called a vertex. The vertex is included in the name of an angle. The angle shown can be named angle A (∠A), angle BAC (∠BAC), or angle CAB(∠CAB).

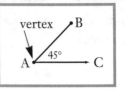

Related word angular

Tools of the Trade

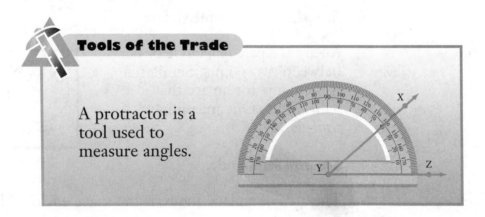

A protractor is a tool used to measure angles.

apex

The apex of a cone or pyramid is the highest point in relation to the base.

See also cone; pyramid.

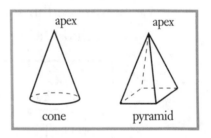

approximate

Approximate means almost exact, or near.

Example
The approximate number of fans the New Orleans Superdome can hold at one time is 95,000.

The approximate height of Shaquille O'Neal, a famous basketball player, is 7 feet. His approximate weight is 300 pounds.

Related words approximately, approximation
See also about.

approximate number

An approximate number is a number that is close to but not exactly equal to another number.

approximate number
(continued)

Example

Chad saw this sign at the candy store: 3 candy bars for $1.00. At this rate, what was the cost of each candy bar?

$1.00 ÷ 3 is a little more than $ .33 and a little less than $ .34.

Both $ .33 and $ .34 are approximate numbers for the cost of each bar.

In this case, Chad paid $ .34 for one candy bar.

See also about; approximate.

arc

An arc is a part of a circle or curve between two points. Semicircle is the name for an arc that is a half-circle. (One meaning of *semi-* is "half.")

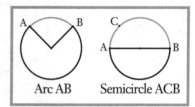

Arc AB   Semicircle ACB

See also semicircle.

area

The area of a plane figure is the space enclosed by that figure.

Area is also the measure of the enclosed space. Area is expressed in square units.

To find the area of plane figures:

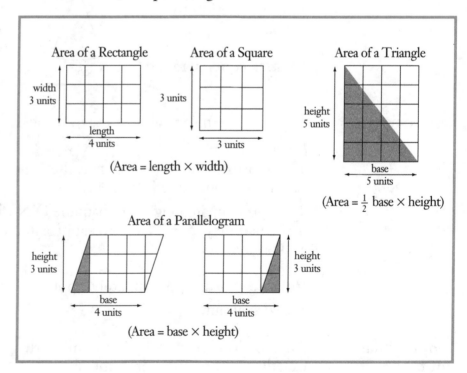

Area of a Rectangle
width 3 units
length 4 units
(Area = length × width)

Area of a Square
3 units
3 units

Area of a Triangle
height 5 units
base 5 units
(Area = ½ base × height)

Area of a Parallelogram
height 3 units
base 4 units
height 3 units
base 4 units
(Area = base × height)

See also cm²; ft²; in.²; km²; m²; mi²; square unit; yd².

14

arithmetic

Arithmetic is the branch of mathematics that deals with the use of one or more of the basic operations on numbers. These basic operations are addition, subtraction, multiplication, and division.

See also addition; basic operations; division; multiplication; operation; subtraction.

arithmetic mean

The arithmetic mean of a set of numbers is an average. To find the arithmetic mean, first find the sum of the set of numbers, then divide by the number of numbers in the set.

See also average.

arithmetic sequence

An arithmetic sequence is a number pattern in which the difference between any two consecutive numbers is the same. Also called arithmetic progression.

Example
3, 7, 11, 15, 19, . . . is an arithmetic sequence.
The difference between any two consecutive numbers is 4.

See also pattern.

array

An array is an orderly arrangement of objects or numbers. Arrays in the shape of a rectangle are often used to model multiplication.

1 × 12   6 × 2

2 × 6   4 × 3

associative property

The associative property means that changing the grouping of the numbers used in an operation does not change the result of that operation. Addition and multiplication have the associative property, but subtraction and division do not. Also called grouping property.

See also associative property of addition; associative property of multiplication.

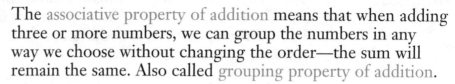

A

associative property of addition

The associative property of addition means that when adding three or more numbers, we can group the numbers in any way we choose without changing the order—the sum will remain the same. Also called grouping property of addition.

Example
6 + 3 + 7 =   6 + 3 + 7 =
(6 + 3) + 7 = 6 + (3 + 7) =
9 + 7 = 16   6 + 10 = 16

The associative property of addition is written with symbols as $(a + b) + c = a + (b + c)$

See also associative property of multiplication.

associative property of multiplication

The associative property of multiplication means that when multiplying three or more numbers, we can group the numbers in any way we choose without changing the order—the product will remain the same. Also called grouping property of multiplication.

Example
4 × 2 × 5=   4 × 2 × 5 =
(4 × 2) × 5 = 4 × (2 × 5) =
8 × 5 = 40   4 × 10 = 40

The associative property of multiplication is written with symbols as $(a \times b) \times c = a \times (b \times c)$

See also associative property of addition.

attribute

The attributes of an object are its characteristics, or qualities. Some attributes can best be described with words, others by counting, and others by measuring. Also called property.

average

The average is a single number used to represent a set of numbers. We use three kinds of averages: the arithmetic mean (usually called the mean), the median, and the mode.

mean The mean is the most familiar kind of average. Also called arithmetic mean.

Example
Cheryl earned the following points on math tests:
(88, 88, 43, 96, 85).
To find the mean, find the total points
scored (88 + 88 + 43 + 96 + 85 = 400).

average
(continued)

Then divide the total points by the number of tests taken (400 ÷ 5 = 80).
The mean of Cheryl's test scores is 80.

median The median is the middle number for a set of data when the data is ordered from least to greatest or greatest to least.

Example
To find the median of Cheryl's test scores, arrange the points in numerical order (43, 85, 88, 88, 96). The median is the middle number, 88.

mode The mode for a set of numbers is the number or numbers that occur most often.

Example
The mode for Cheryl's test scores is 88 because it occurs twice, and each of the other scores occurs only once.

Related words averaged; averaging

See also mean; median; mode

Did You Know?

The average length of a human lifetime in the United States is nearly 80 years. In the United States the average amount of time per person spent with media entertainment is about 3350 hours each year. (Of this time, about 1000 hours are spent watching network television.

axis

pl. **axes** An axis is a reference line in a coordinate system. The *x*- and *y*-axes are marked in this coordinate system.

See also coordinate system; *x*- ; *y*-axes.

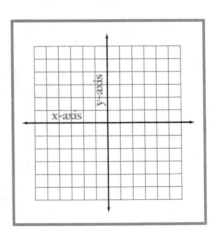

bar graph

A bar graph is a kind of graph that uses rectangular bars to show information. Bar graphs are useful in comparing categories or groups of information. A bar graph can also be formed with real objects, pictures, or symbols.

The data on a bar graph can be presented either vertically or horizontally. Notice that the same information is represented in both graphs.

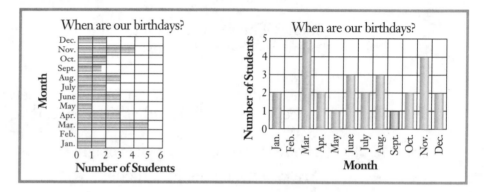

double bar graph A double bar graph presents two sets of data on the same graph.

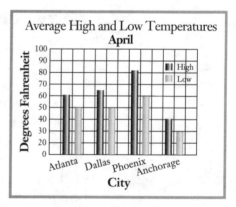

real graph A real graph is a kind of bar graph that uses the real objects being graphed.

bar graph
(continued)

picture graph A picture graph is a kind of bar graph that uses pictures or drawings to represent data.

Our Favorite Sports	
Baseball	⊖ ⊖ ⊖ ⊖
Football	⊖ ⊖
Soccer	⊖ ⊖ ⊖
Bowling	⊖ ⊖
Dance	⊖ ⊖ ⊖ ⊖
Other	⊖

⊖ = 2 students

symbolic graph A symbolic graph uses a symbol such as X or O or the blocks on the graph to show information.

Most bar graphs are symbolic graphs.

Seedling's Growth	
June	✔
July	✔✔
August	✔✔✔
September	✔✔✔✔✔
October	✔✔✔✔✔✔✔

Each ✔ = 2cm

See also line plot; scale.

base

A base of a geometric figure is a side or face on which the figure can rest.

Examples

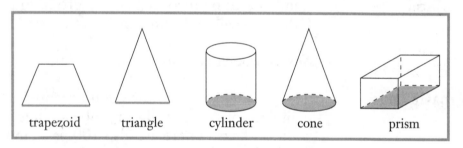

trapezoid   triangle   cylinder   cone   prism

The base of a numeration system is the number that is used to build the place value of that system.

Our decimal numeration system is a base-ten system.

The base of an exponent is a number that is raised to a power.

Base Ten				
10,000	1000	100	10	1
10^4	10^3	10^2	10^1	10^0
6	5	0	0	0

The Cougar Stadium holds 65,000 people.

In 10^2, 10 is the base and 2 is the exponent.
10 is raised to the power of 2.
($10^2 = 10 \times 10 = 100$)

See also decimal numeration system; exponent; power of a number.

B

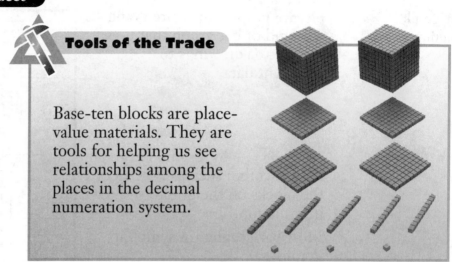

Tools of the Trade

Base-ten blocks are place-value materials. They are tools for helping us see relationships among the places in the decimal numeration system.

See also decimal numeration system.

base-ten numeration system

The base-ten numeration system is a system of grouping by tens. For example, when 9 ones have been counted, the next number will be recorded as one group of tens and zero ones (10). Also called decimal numeration system.

See also decimal numeration system.

basic facts

The basic facts are all the addition and multiplication combinations of one-digit numbers. There are 100 basic addition facts. There are also 100 basic multiplication facts. Also called basic number facts.

Addition Table of Basic Facts

+	0	1	2	3	4	5	6	7	8	9
0	0	1	2	3	4	5	6	7	8	9
1	1	2	3	4	5	6	7	8	9	10
2	2	3	4	5	6	7	8	9	10	11
3	3	4	5	6	7	8	9	10	11	12
4	4	5	6	7	8	9	10	11	12	13
5	5	6	7	8	9	10	11	12	13	14
6	6	7	8	9	10	11	12	13	14	15
7	7	8	9	10	11	12	13	14	15	16
8	8	9	10	11	12	13	14	15	16	17
9	9	10	11	12	13	14	15	16	17	18

Multiplication Table of Basic Facts

×	0	1	2	3	4	5	6	7	8	9
0	0	0	0	0	0	0	0	0	0	0
1	0	1	2	3	4	5	6	7	8	9
2	0	2	4	6	8	10	12	14	16	18
3	0	3	6	9	12	15	18	21	24	27
4	0	4	8	12	16	20	24	28	32	36
5	0	5	10	15	20	25	30	35	40	45
6	0	6	12	18	24	30	36	42	48	54
7	0	7	14	21	28	35	42	49	56	63
8	0	8	16	24	32	40	48	56	64	72
9	0	9	18	27	36	45	54	63	72	81

$4 + 5 = 9$ $5 + 4 = 9$ $3 \times 7 = 21$ $7 \times 3 = 21$

See also commutative property of addition; commutative property of multiplication; fact family.

basic operations

The four basic operations of arithmetic are addition, subtraction, multiplication, and division.

See also addition; arithmetic; basic facts; division; multiplication; operation; subtraction.

benchmark

A benchmark is a reference point that can be used to help in making an estimate

Example
The width of a child's pinkie finger is a good benchmark for a centimeter.

billion

A billion is equal to 1,000 millions. In standard form, one billion is written as 1,000,000,000.
With an exponent, one billion may be written as 1×10^9 (or simply as 10^9).

See also decimal numeration system.

bisect

To bisect is to divide into two parts that have the same size and shape.

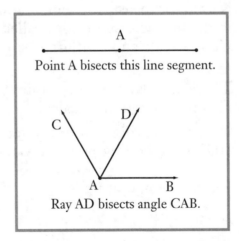

Point A bisects this line segment.

Ray AD bisects angle CAB.

Related words bisector; bisecting lines

capacity

Capacity usually refers to the amount of liquid a container can hold. It may be reported in units of liquid measure. Capacity is also used in other ways. For example, an elevator may have a capacity of 13 people or 2100 pounds.

See also cup; gallon; kiloliter; liter; metric system of measurement; milliliter; pint; quart; tablespoon; teaspoon.

cardinal number

A cardinal number is a whole number that tells how many are in a group. For example, there are 4 children in that family.

Cartesian coordinate system

The Cartesian coordinate system is a system used to locate points in a plane relative to the intersection of 2 perpendicular lines, or *axes*, in the plane.

See also coordinate system; *x*-axis; *y*-axis.

Celsius (°C) temperature scale

The Celsius (°C) temperature scale is used for measuring temperature in the metric system. Also called Celsius scale and centigrade scale.

There are two reference points for this temperature scale:

0° is the freezing point of water
100° is the boiling point of water

See also temperature.

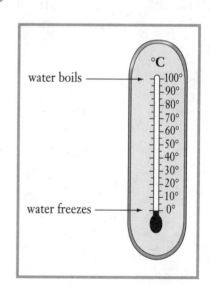

center of a circle

The center of a circle is a point inside a circle from which all points on the circle are an equal distance

See also circle.

centi-

Centi- is a prefix meaning "one hundredth."
1 centimeter = 0.01 meter
1 centiliter = 0.01 liter
1 centigram = 0.01 gram

centigrade scale

The centigrade scale is a name sometimes used for the Celsius temperature scale. The name *centigrade* comes from the 100 degrees, or units, between the freezing and boiling points of water. Also called Celsius (°C) temperature scale.

See also Celsius (°C) temperature scale.

centigram (cg)

A centigram is a unit of weight in the metric system of measurement. 100 centigrams = 1 gram

See also metric system of measurement.

centiliter (cL)

A centiliter is a unit of capacity in the metric system of measurement. 100 centiliters = 1 liter

See also metric system of measurement.

centimeter (cm)

A centimeter is a unit of length in the metric system of measurement. 100 centimeters = 1 meter

See also metric system of measurement.

century

A century is a measure of time.
1 century = 100 years

Did You Know?

The United States has been a country for about two centuries. The oldest country in the world is China, which has a recorded history of about 30 centuries.

chance

Chance is the likelihood that a given event will occur. Also called probability.

See also probability.

chart

A chart is a form used to record information.

chord

A chord is any line segment with both endpoints on a circle.

diameter The diameter, a special kind of chord, passes through the center of a circle.

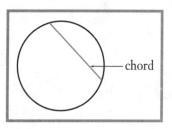

See also diameter.

circle

A circle is a closed plane figure with all points the same distance from a point called the center.

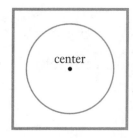

circle graph

A circle graph is a graph in the shape of a circle, or pie, that shows how a total amount has been divided into parts. Also called pie graph.

The circle represents the total amount. The slices of "pie" show how the total amount has been divided.

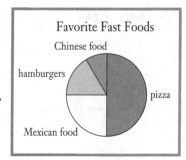

See also bar graph; line graph.

circumference

Circumference is the distance around a circle. The distance around any circle is a little more than three times its diameter.

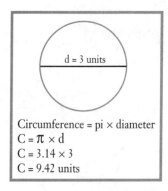

Circumference = pi × diameter
$C = \pi \times d$
$C = 3.14 \times 3$
$C = 9.42$ units

pi (π) The actual ratio of the circumference of a circle to its diameter is known as pi. The approximate value of pi is 3.14.

To find the circumference (C) of a circle, multiply the diameter (d) of the circle by 3.14 (an approximation of pi).

The formula for finding the circumference of a circle may be written as: $C = \pi \times d$.

See also perimeter; pi.

clockwise	Clockwise is the direction in which the hands of a clock move. They pass the numbers on the clock face in order from least to greatest.	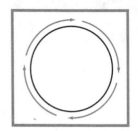

See also counterclockwise.

closed curve

Also called closed figure. A closed curve is a curve that starts and stops at the same place.

simple closed curves A simple closed curve is a closed curve that does not cross itself. In the drawing the two curves are simple closed curves.

clustering

Clustering is a method used for estimating a result when numbers appear to group, or cluster, around a common number.

Example
Juan bought decorations for a party. He spent $3.63 for balloons, $3.85 for party favors, and $4.55 for streamers. About how much did he spend for decorations?
$3.63, $3.85, and $4.55 cluster around $4.
4 + 4 + 4 = 12 (or 3 × 4 = 12)
Juan spent about $12 for party decorations.

See also estimation strategies.

cm²

Read as square centimeter. A cm² is equal to the area of a square that measures 1 centimeter on each side. Also written as square centimeter.

See also square; square unit.

cm³

Read as cubic centimeter. A cm³ is equal to the volume of a cube that measures 1 cm in length, 1 cm in width, and 1 cm in height. Also written as cubic centimeter.

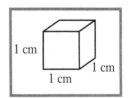

See also cube; cubic unit.

column

A column is a vertical arrangement of items or numbers from top to bottom in an array or table.

See also table.

Year	Number of Missions With Astronauts	New Astronauts in Space (first space flight)	Time in Space
1961	🧑🧑	🧑🧑	30 minutes
1962	🧑🧑🧑	🧑🧑🧑	19 hours
1963	🧑	🧑	34 hours
1964			0
1965	🧑🧑🧑🧑🧑	🧑🧑🧑🧑🧑	330 hours
1966	🧑🧑🧑🧑🧑	🧑🧑🧑🧑	309 hours
1967			0
1968	🧑🧑	🧑🧑🧑	407 hours
1969	🧑🧑🧑🧑	🧑🧑🧑	873 hours
1970	🧑	🧑🧑	141 hours
1971	🧑🧑	🧑🧑🧑	511 hours
1972	🧑🧑	🧑🧑🧑	568 hours
1973	🧑🧑🧑	🧑🧑🧑🧑🧑	171 days

↑
column

common denominator

A common denominator is a common multiple of the denominators of two or more fractions. Two of the common denominators for $\frac{1}{6}$ and $\frac{3}{8}$ are 24 and 48.

See also least common denominator.

common factor

A common factor is a factor that two or more numbers share. Also called common divisor.

Example
Factors of 10: 1, 2, 5, and 10
Factors of 20: 1, 2, 4, 5, 10, and 20
Common factors of 10 and 20 include 1, 2, 5, and 10.

See also greatest common factor.

common fraction

A common fraction is one way of expressing a fractional number. (Decimal fractions and percents are two other ways of expressing fractional numbers.) Also called fraction.

part of a whole or set A common fraction may name a part of a whole or a set.

Example
$\frac{3}{4}$ of the chocolate pie is left.
$\frac{3}{4}$ is a common fraction naming a part of the whole pie.

common fraction
(continued)

division Common fractions are also used to express division.

Example
Nancy wants to make omelets for breakfast. She has 6 eggs.
She needs 2 eggs for each omelet. How many omelets can
she make?
$$\frac{6}{2} = 3$$
Nancy can make 3 omelets.

ratio A common fraction can be used to name a ratio.

Example
Dante, Karen, Matt, and Andy baked cupcakes for the party.
They baked enough for each guest to have 2 cupcakes.

The ratio of guests to cupcakes can be expressed as the
common fraction $\frac{1}{2}$ (or as the ratio 1:2).

For each guest, there are 2 cupcakes.

The ratio could also be expressed as the common fraction $\frac{2}{1}$
(or as the ratio 2:1). There are 2 cupcakes for each guest.

See also fraction; fractional number; rational number.

common multiple

A common multiple is a multiple that two or more
numbers share.
Example
Multiples of 4: 4, 8, 12, 16, 20, 24, . . .
Multiples of 8: 8, 16, 24, . . .

Some of the common multiples of 4 and 8 are 8, 16, and 24.

least common multiple (LCM) The least common multiple is
the smallest whole-number multiple other than 0 that two
or more numbers share.

The least common multiple of 4 and 8 is 8.
This is written as LCM (4, 8) = 8.

See also least common multiple; multiple.

commutative property

The commutative property means that changing the order of the two numbers used in an operation does not change the result of that operation. Addition and multiplication have the commutative property, but subtraction and division do not. Also called order property.

See also commutative property of addition; commutative property of multiplication.

commutative property of addition

The commutative property of addition means that the order in which two numbers are added does not change the sum. Also called order property of addition.

Examples

$7 + 9 = 16$ $\frac{1}{4} + \frac{1}{2} = \frac{3}{4}$

$9 + 7 = 16$ $\frac{1}{2} + \frac{1}{4} = \frac{3}{4}$

The commutative property of addition is written with symbols as $a + b = b + a$.

See also commutative property of multiplication.

commutative property of multiplication

The commutative property of multiplication means that changing the order in which two numbers are multiplied does not change the product. Also called order property of multiplication.

Examples

$8 \times 5 = 40$ $1.3 \times 4 = 5.2$ $5 \times 8 = 40$ $4 \times 1.3 = 5.2$

The commutative property of multiplication is written with symbols as $a \times b = b \times a$.

See also commutative property of addition.

compass

A compass is a tool that can be used to draw circles and arcs and to copy line segments. Many plane figures can be constructed with only a compass and a straightedge.

A hexagon can be drawn within a circle using a compass and a straight-edge. Another kind of compass is used as a tool for finding directions.

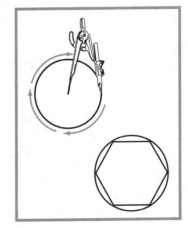

See also straightedge.

compatible numbers

Compatible numbers are numbers that seem to "go together." They are easy to compute mentally. The use of compatible numbers is an estimation strategy.

Example
Bob bought a package of 4 pairs of athletic socks for $10.99. About how much did he pay for each pair?

$10.99 is close to $12.00 (12 is a multiple of 4).
12 ÷ 4 = 3 Each pair of socks cost about $3.00.

See also estimation strategies.

complete factorization

Complete factorization is the expression of a composite number as the product of its prime factors. Also called prime factorization.

See also prime factorization.

composite number

A composite number is a whole number with more than two factors.

Example
16 is a composite number. Its factors are 1, 2, 4, 8, and 16.
These arrays for 16 show its factors.

compound event

A compound event is two or more independent events considered together.

independent events Independent events are events that have no effect on each other.

Example
You are playing a game in which you are rolling two dice. You score if the sum of your dice is an even number.

The result of the roll of one die does not affect the result of the roll of the other die. Rolling one die and rolling the other

compound event
(continued)

die are two independent events. The results of both dice are considered together to determine if you rolled an even number. This is a compound event.

computation

Computation is doing the arithmetic operations needed to solve a problem.

Related words compute, computer

See also basic operations; mental computation.

cone

A cone is a space figure that usually has a circular base. It comes to a point on the end opposite the base.

apex The point, or vertex, is called the apex.

Related word conical

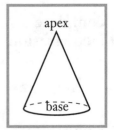

congruent figures

Congruent figures are figures that have the same size and shape.

Examples
These figures below are congruent because they are the same size and shape.

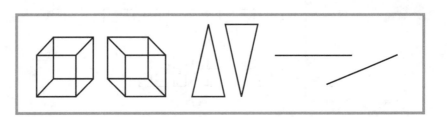

Did You Know?

Identical twins have congruent, or almost congruent, features.

construction

A construction is a drawing of a geometric figure made by using only a compass and a straightedge.

Tools of the Trade

A compass is used for drawing circles and arcs and for copying line segments. The straightedge is used for drawing line segments.

See also compass; straightedge.

coordinates

Coordinates in a plane are the two items in an ordered pair, used to identify a location on a map or in a plane coordinate system relative to a fixed point or *origin*.

Examples
Often maps will use a letter as one of the coordinates for locating a point and a numeral for the other. The coordinates of Brussels, Belgium, on this map are B and 2.

The coordinates of this point are 6 and 4. The first coordinate, 6, is the *x*-coordinate. The second coordinate, 4, is the *y*-coordinate.

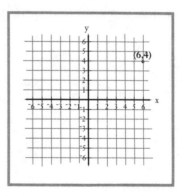

See also coordinate system.

coordinate system

A coordinate system is a system used for locating points on a plane.

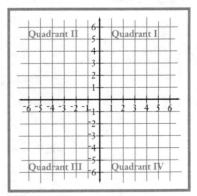

When used to locate points on a plane, also called Cartesian coordinate system and rectangular coordinate system.

x-axis The *x*-axis is the horizontal number line.

y-axis The *y*-axis is the vertical number line.

origin The origin is the point of intersection of the *x*- and *y*-axes.

quadrant The *x*- and *y*-axes divide the coordinate system into four sections, or quadrants. They are numbered in order from I to IV, starting in the upper right quadrant and going counterclockwise.

ordered pair A point is named by an ordered pair. The ordered pair also tells its location in the coordinate system.

x-coordinate The first number in the ordered pair is called the *x*-coordinate. It indicates a distance along the *x*-axis.

y-coordinate The second number in the ordered pair is called the *y*-coordinate. It indicates a distance along the *y*-axis.

plotting a point Plotting a point, or locating and marking a point when given its coordinates, is described in these examples.

Examples
To plot (2,1), first locate 2 on the *x*-axis and 1 on the *y*-axis. *Follow the arrows shown in the drawing.* Because both coordinates are positive numbers, the point is located in Quadrant I.

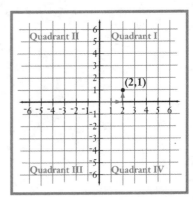

coordinate system
(continued

To plot (⁻4,⁻3), first locate ⁻4 on the *x*-axis and ⁻3 on the *y*-axis. *Follow the arrows shown in the drawing.* Because both coordinates are negative numbers, the point is located in Quadrant III.

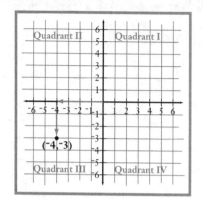

counterclockwise

Counterclockwise is the direction opposite the way the hands of a clock move.

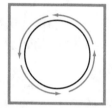

**counting
numbers**

Counting numbers are the numbers 1, 2, 3, 4, 5, and so on. They go on without end. Counting numbers are used to name the number in a set of objects. Also called natural numbers.

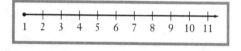

**counting
principle**

The counting principle is a way to find the possible choices or outcomes in situations where order is important. Also called basic counting principle and fundamental counting principle.

Examples
There are 3 kinds of sandwiches and 2 flavors of ice cream in the refrigerator. You may choose one kind of sandwich and then one flavor of ice cream for lunch. How many different choices do you have for lunch?

3 (sandwiches) × 2 (flavors of ice cream) = 6
There are 6 choices.

A coin is tossed 3 times. Each outcome is either heads or tails. How many different outcomes are possible?

2 = number of possible outcomes for the first toss
2 = number of possible outcomes for the second toss
2 = number of possible outcomes for the third toss
2 × 2 × 2 = 8
8 different outcomes are possible.

See also tree diagram.

cube

In geometry, also called hexahedron. A cube is a space figure with 6 square faces that are all the same size. It is one of the five regular polyhedra.

The cube of a number is that number used as a factor 3 times.

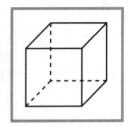

Examples
$2^3 = 2 \times 2 \times 2 = 8$
$10^3 = 10 \times 10 \times 10 = 1000$

Related words cubic, cuboid
See also polyhedron.

cubic centimeter (cm³)

A cubic centimeter is equal to the volume of a cube that measures 1 centimeter on each edge.

See also cubic unit; cm³.

cubic decimeter (dm³)

A cubic decimeter is equal to the volume of a cube that measures 1 decimeter (10 cm) on each edge.

See also cubic unit; dm³.

cubic foot (ft³)

A cubic foot is equal to the volume of a cube that measures 1 foot on each edge.

See also cubic unit; ft³.

cubic inch (in.³)

A cubic inch is equal to the volume of a cube that measures 1 inch on each edge. An ice cube is about the size of 1 in.³.

See also cubic unit; in.³.

cubic meter (m³)

A cubic meter is equal to the volume of a cube that measures 1 meter on each edge.

See also cubic unit; m³.

cubic unit

A cubic unit is a unit for measuring volume. Each face of a cubic unit is a square, and each edge is one unit in length.

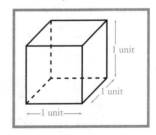

cubic yard (yd³)

A cubic yard is equal to the volume of a cube that measures 1 yard on each edge.

In the metric system, cubic units include cm³ (cubic centimeter), dm³ (cubic decimeter), and m³ (cubic meter).

 Did You Know?

Although a cubic unit of volume is usually thought of in the shape of a cube, it can also take other shapes. For example, a cubic yard of concrete may be poured and spread a few inches deep to form a small patio.

See also customary system of measurement; metric system of measurement.

cup (C)

A cup is a unit of capacity in the customary system of measurement.
2 cups = 1 pint

See also capacity; customary system of measurement.

customary system of measurement

The customary system of measurement is the measurement system used most commonly in everyday life in the United States. The customary system was brought to this land by colonists from England. Many cultures, some of them dating back to ancient times, contributed to its development. The customary system includes units for measuring length, weight, capacity, area, volume, and temperature. Also called customary system, customary measurement system, English measurement system, English system of measurement, standard system of measurement, and U.S. Customary System.

length The most common units for measuring length in the customary system include inch (in.), foot (ft), yard (yd), and mile (mi).

12 in. = 1 ft
3 ft = 1 yd
5280 ft or 1760 yd = 1 mi

weight The most common units for measuring weight in the customary system include ounce (oz), pound (lb), and ton (T).

16 oz = 1 lb   2000 lb = 1 T

**customary system
of measurement**
(continued)

capacity Commonly used units for measuring capacity in the customary system include teaspoon (t), tablespoon (T), cup (C), pint (pt), quart (qt), and gallon (gal).

3 t = 1 T   2 pt = 1 qt
16 T = 1 C   4 qt = 1 gal
2 C = 1 pt

Fluid ounces (fl oz) are also used for measuring capacity.

1 fl oz = 2 T   16 fl oz = 1 pt
8 fl oz = 1 C   32 fl oz = 1 qt

area Square units are used for measuring area. In the customary system these include in.^{2}, ft^2, and yd^2.

144 in.^{2} = 1 ft^2 9 ft^2 = 1 yd^2

Acres and mi^2 are also used for measuring area.

1 acre = 43,560 ft^2 640 acres = 1 mi^2

volume Cubic units are used for measuring volume. In the customary system these include in.^{3}, ft^3, and yd^3.

1728 in.^{3} = 1 ft^3 27 ft^3 = 1 yd^3

temperature The Fahrenheit (°F) scale is used for measuring temperature in the customary system. Two reference points for this temperature scale are
32° the freezing point of water
212° the boiling point of water

See also area; capacity; cubic unit; cup; Fahrenheit (°F) temperature scale; fluid ounce; foot; ft^2; ft^3; gallon; in.^{2}; in.^{3}; inch; length; metric system of measurement; mi^2; mile; ounce; pint; pound; quart; square unit; tablespoon; teaspoon; temperature; ton; volume; weight; yd^2; yd^3; yard.

cylinder

A cylinder is a space figure with two parallel bases (usually circles) that are the same size. A tracing of the net on the right can be cut and taped to form a cylinder.

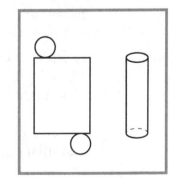

Related word cylindrical

data

Singular **datum** Data are facts or information gathered for a purpose. Data may be in the form of either words or numbers.

This sign gives us information, or data, about the movies being shown. The names of the movies and their ratings are in words or letters. The times are shown as numbers.

1001 FRENCH POODLES
G 7:15 9:30

PROM QUEEN
PG 7:00 9:15

statistics The branch of mathematics called statistics provides us with tools for organizing, representing, analyzing, and interpreting data. Data are often displayed in tables and graphs.

See also statistics.

1995 Standard of Living Indicators	China	U.S.A.
People per telephone	36.4	1.3
People per television set	6.7	1.2
Literacy	78%	97%
Children per woman	1.84	2.08
Life expectancy in years	68.08	75.99

1995 Female Earnings per Male Dollar

15-24	96¢
25-34	84¢
35-44	72¢
45-54	62¢
55-64	63¢
65 and over	67¢

deca-

Deca- is a prefix meaning "ten." Also spelled deka-.

See also deka-.

decade

A decade is a measure of time equal to 10 years.

Did You Know?

Decade comes from a Greek word meaning "ten." Other words that share the same root include *decathlon* and *decagon*.

decagon

A decagon is a polygon with 10 sides (Deca- means "ten.")

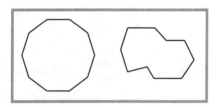

deci-

Deci- is a prefix meaning "one tenth."
1 decimeter = 0.1 meter
1 deciliter = 0.1 liter
1 decigram = 0.1 gram

decigram (dg)

A decigram is a unit of weight in the metric system of measurement.
10 decigrams = 1 gram

See also metric system of measurement.

deciliter (dL)

A deciliter is a unit of capacity in the metric system of measurement.
10 deciliters = 1 liter

See also metric system of measurement.

decimal

Decimal means "based on ten." The numeration system we use most of the time is called the decimal numeration system because it is based on groupings of ten. Decimal is also used as another name for decimal fraction and decimal mixed number.

See also decimal fraction; decimal mixed number; decimal numeration system.

decimal fraction

A decimal fraction is a fractional number with a denominator of ten or a power of ten. (Common fractions, percents, and decimal fractions are all ways of expressing fractional numbers.) Also called decimal.

Examples

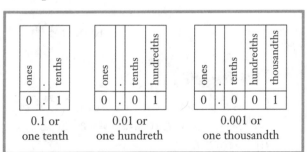

ones	.	tenths
0	.	1

0.1 or one tenth

ones	.	tenths	hundredths
0	.	0	1

0.01 or one hundreth

ones	.	tenths	hundredths	thousandths
0	.	0	0	1

0.001 or one thousandth

0.8 (or $\frac{8}{10}$)

| **decimal fraction** (continued) | Each of the place-value charts shows a decimal fraction. Decimal fractions are usually written with a decimal point. A decimal fraction can also be expressed as a common fraction with a denominator of ten or a power of ten. |

Examples

$0.1 = \frac{1}{10}$ $0.001 = \frac{1}{1000}$

$0.01 = \frac{1}{100}$ $0.56 = \frac{56}{100}$

See also decimal numeration system.

decimal mixed number

A decimal mixed number is made up of a whole number and a decimal fraction. Also called decimal.

Example
4.4 inches of rain fell in June, and 1.05 inches fell in July.
4.4 and 1.05 are decimal mixed numbers.

Money amounts are expressed in decimal mixed numbers.

Example
Jerry's baseball cap cost $8.95.
8.95 is a decimal mixed number.

decimal numeration system

The decimal numeration system is a system for expressing the value of numbers based on grouping by tens. Also called base-ten numeration system and Hindu-Arabic numeration system.

Each place in the decimal numeration system has a value that is a power of 10.

Whole Numbers											
Billions			Millions			Thousands			Ones		
hundreds	tens	ones	hundreds	tens	ones	hundreds	tens	ones	hundreds	tens	ones
10^{11}	10^{10}	10^{9}	10^{8}	10^{7}	10^{6}	10^{5}	10^{4}	10^{3}	10^{2}	10^{1}	10^{0}

This chart can be continued to the left for writing larger whole numbers than those shown. It can also be continued to the right for writing smaller numbers, called decimal fractions.

Decimal Fractions							
ones	.	tenths	hundredths	thousandths	ten-thousandths	hundred-thousandths	millionths
10^{0}	.	10^{-1}	10^{-2}	10^{-3}	10^{-4}	10^{-5}	10^{-6}

See also decimal fraction; place value.

decimal point

A decimal point is the dot used in writing a decimal fraction or a decimal mixed number. In a decimal mixed number, the decimal point separates the whole number from the decimal fraction.

In decimal fractions, 0 is often written before the decimal point.

Examples
0.4   Read as four tenths
0.003 Read as three thousandths

In decimal mixed numbers, the decimal point is read as *and*.

Examples
1.3   Read as one and three tenths
4.58 Read as four and fifty-eight hundredths

A special use of decimal fractions and decimal mixed numbers is in expressing amounts of money. In money the decimal point is used to separate dollars and cents.

Examples
$ .59 Read as fifty-nine cents
$2.34 Read as two dollars and thirty-four cents

decimeter (dm)

A decimeter is a unit of length in the metric system of measurement.
10 decimeters = 1 meter

See also metric system of measurement.

degree (°)

Degree is the name used for the basic units of measurement for angles and temperature.

angles Five degrees (5°) are shown by the angle in the drawing.

There are 360 degrees (360°) in a circle.

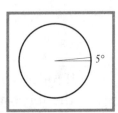

The measure of the angle shown is 80°.

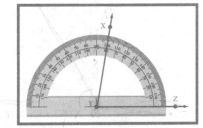

degree (continued)

temperature One degree of temperature on the Celsius scale is equal to 1.8 degrees of temperature on the Fahrenheit scale.

degrees Celsius (°C) The Celsius temperature scale measures temperature in degrees Celsius (°C).

Freezing temperature for water is 0°C.
Boiling temperature for water is 100°C.

degrees Fahrenheit (°F)
The Fahrenheit temperature scale measures temperature in degrees Fahrenheit (°F).

Freezing temperature for water is 32°F.

Boiling temperature for water is 212°F.

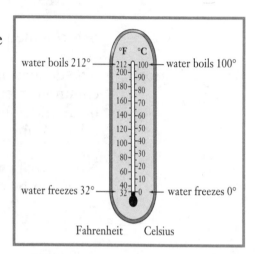

See also angle, Celsius (°C) temperature scale; Fahrenheit (°F) temperature scale.

deka-

Deka- is a prefix meaning "ten." Also spelled deca-.
1 dekameter = 10 meters
1 dekaliter = 10 liters
1 dekagram = 10 grams

dekagram (dag)

A dekagram is a unit of weight in the metric system of measurement. Also spelled decagram.
1 dekagram = 10 grams

See also metric system of measurement.

dekaliter (daL)

A dekaliter is a unit of capacity in the metric system of measurement. Also spelled decaliter.
1 dekaliter = 10 liters

See also metric system of measurement.

dekameter (dam)

A dekameter is a unit of length in the metric system of measurement. Also spelled decameter.

1 dekameter = 10 meters

Did You Know?

Many classrooms are about 1 dekameter wide.

See also metric system of measurement.

denominator

The denominator is the name of one of the two terms of a common fraction. It is the part of the fraction that tells how many fractional parts there are in the whole or set. It also has other meanings. For example, it is the second term in a ratio.

Notice that the denominator is written below the fraction bar.

$$\frac{3 \text{ numerator}}{4 \text{ denominator}}$$

Example
In this picture, $\frac{1}{2}$ is the fraction represented and 2 is the denominator of the fraction.

See also numerator.

dependent event

A dependent event has an outcome that is affected by the outcome of a previous event.

Example
You have only three coins in your bank. You know that they are a quarter, a dime, and a nickel. You shake out one coin, a quarter. You do not put it back. What coins are left to shake out next time? In this situation, shaking out a second coin is a dependent event, because the outcome depends on which coin you shook out the first time.

diagonal

For a polygon a diagonal is a line segment joining two vertices that are not next to each other. All the diagonals are shown for the two polygons on the right.

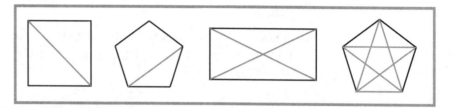

For a polyhedron a diagonal is a line segment joining two vertices that are in different faces.

One diagonal is shown for this polyhedron.

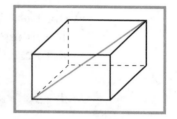

 Did You Know?

The diagonal beams in this bridge help make it strong.

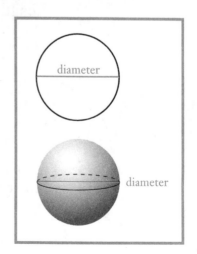

diameter

The diameter of a circle is a line segment that passes through the center of the circle and has endpoints on the circle.

The diameter of a sphere is a line segment that passes through the center of the sphere and has endpoints on the sphere.

diameter

diameter

difference

The difference is the result of subtraction when two numbers are compared. It answers the question "How many more (or less) are there?"

Example
The soccer game was very close. Alice's team scored 9 points, and Wanda's team scored 8 points. How many more points did Alice's team score?
9 - 8 = 1
The difference in the scores of the teams was 1 point.

digit

A digit is a basic symbol used in a numeration system. The ten digits used in our decimal, or base-ten, numeration system are 0, 1, 2, 3, 4, 5, 6, 7, 8, and 9.

Did You Know?

Fingers and toes are also called digits. Perhaps the reason for a numeration system based on ten is that humans have 10 fingers!

dimension

The dimensions of some plane figures are length and width. The dimensions of some space figures are length, width, and height. For some geometric figures, the dimensions are also the lengths of sides or edges. A line segment has only one demension—length.

Example
The dimensions of this rectangular prism are

Length   3 centimeters
Width   2 centimeters
Height   1 centimeters

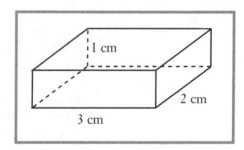

discount

A discount is an amount the regular price of an item has been reduced. Discounts can be expressed as dollar amounts, common fractions, or percents.

Example
The discount on the bicycle is $25. It now costs $75.

discount (continued) The discount on the bicycle is $\frac{1}{4}$ ($25) off its regular price. It now costs $75.

The discount on the bicycle is 25% ($25) off its regular price. It now costs $75.00

distributive property of multiplication over addition

The distributive property of multiplication over addition can be expressed as $a(b + c) = (a \times b) + (a \times c)$.

Example
$a(b + c) = (a \times b) + (a \times c)$
$3(4 + 2) = (3 \times 4) + (3 \times 2)$
It can be used to figure out harder multiplication facts. It uses easier multiplication facts.

Examples
$3 \times 8 =$
$3 \times (4 + 4) =$
$(3 \times 4) + (3 \times 4) =$
$12 + 12 =$
24

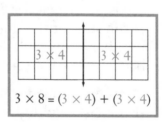

$3 \times 8 = (3 \times 4) + (3 \times 4)$

$4 \times 9 =$
$(4 \times 5) + (4 \times 4) =$
$20 + 16 =$
36

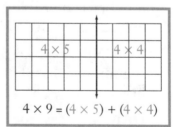

$4 \times 9 = (4 \times 5) + (4 \times 4)$

The distributive property of multiplication over addition is also used in multiplying numbers with more than one digit.

Example

$$
\begin{array}{c}
431 \\
\times\,2 \\
\hline
\end{array}
\qquad
\begin{array}{c}
400 \\
\times\,2 \\
\hline
800
\end{array}
\;+\;
\begin{array}{c}
30 \\
\times\,2 \\
\hline
60
\end{array}
\;+\;
\begin{array}{c}
1 \\
\times\,2 \\
\hline
2
\end{array}
\;=\; 862
$$

divide

One number divides another number if there is no remainder after division.

Example
4 divides 12 because 12 ÷ 4 = 3 with no remainder.

dividend

A dividend is the number being divided.

Example
In 10 ÷ 5 = 2,
10 is the dividend.
5 is the divisor.
2 is the quotient.

divisibility test

A divisibility test is a way of finding out if one number divides another number. Also called divisibility rule.
Divisibility tests for 2, 3, 4, 5, 6, 9, and 10 are included here.

Divisibility test for 2
If a number has an even number in the ones place, it is divisible by 2. For example, 3018 is divisible by 2 because 8 is an even number.

Divisibility test for 3
If the sum of the digits of a number is divisible by 3, the number is divisible by 3. For example, 2310 is divisible by 3 because 2 + 3 + 1 + 0 = 6, a number that is divisible by 3.

Divisibility test for 4
If the last two digits form a number that is divisible by 4, the number is divisible by 4. For example, 8728 is divisible by 4 because 28 is divisible by 4.

Divisibility test for 5
If a number has 0 or 5 in the ones place, it is divisible by 5. For example, 385 and 400 are divisible by 5.

Divisibility test for 6
If a number is divisible by both 2 and 3, it is divisible by 6. For example, 396 is divisible by 6 because it is divisible by both 2 and 3. (The ones place is an even number, making it divisible by 2. The sum of the digits is 18; therefore, it is divisible by 3.)

Divisibility test for 9
If the sum of the digits of a number is divisible by 9, the number is divisible by 9. For example, 198,432 is divisible by 9 because 1 + 9 + 8 + 4 + 3 + 2 = 27, a number that is divisible by 9.

| **Divisibility test** (continued) | **Divisibility test for 10** |

Divisibility test for 10
If a number has 0 in the ones place, it is divisible by 10.
For example, 710 is divisible by 10.

divisible

A number is divisible by another number if the remainder is 0 after dividing.

Example
There are 32 children. Can they form 4 teams with no one being left out?

$$4\overline{)32}$$ = 8 R0

They can form 4 teams with no one being left out because 32 is divisible by 4. (There is no remainder after dividing.)

divides Another way of saying that 32 is divisible by 4 is to say that 4 divides 32. One number divides another number if there is no remainder after division.

division

Division is the inverse, or opposite, operation of multiplication. It "undoes" multiplication.

Example
$6 \times 4 = 24$, so $24 \div 4 = 6$.

In the example $24 \div 4 = 6$,
24 is the dividend.
4 is the divisor.
6 is the quotient.

Written with symbols:
Where c is the dividend, b is the divisor, and a is the quotient,
$c \div b = a$ because $a \times b = c$.

division by zero Note that the divisor b cannot be zero because there is no number a that will multiply b to equal c when $c \neq$ zero.

sharing Division can be used to find the size of a part of a set. This is called sharing, or partition division. When division is used to find the size of a part, a number is divided into equal parts.

There are 12 cookies. They are divided equally among 4 people.

division (continued)

How many cookies does each person get?
12 ÷ 4 = 3
Each person gets 3 cookies.
(The size of each person's part, or share, is 3.)

measurement division Division is also used to find the number of parts in a set. This is called measurement division.

There are 12 cookies. We want to give 4 cookies to each person. How many people will get cookies?

12 ÷ 4 = 3
3 people get cookies. (The set of cookies is divided into 3 parts.)

Related words divide, divides, dividend, divisible, divisive

division sentence

A division sentence is a number sentence used to express division, in which the numbers are usually written the following order: Dividend ÷ divisor = quotient.

Example
15 ÷ 3 = 5

See also number sentence.

divisor

A divisor is the number by which another number is divided.

Example
In 14 ÷ 2 = 7,
14 is the dividend.
2 is the divisor.
7 is the quotient.

dodecagon

A dodecagon is a polygon with 12 sides. (*Do-* means "two" and *deca-* means "ten.")

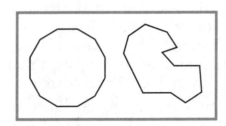

dodecahedron

A dodecahedron is a space figure with 12 faces. If each is in the shape of a regular pentagon, it is one of the five regular polyhedra.

See also polyhedron.

double

A double is an addition fact in which the two addends are the same number.

Example
5 + 5 = 10

Table of Basic Addition Facts

+	0	1	2	3	4	5	6	7	8	9
0	0	1	2	3	4	5	6	7	8	9
1	1	2	3	4	5	6	7	8	9	10
2	2	3	4	5	6	7	8	9	10	11
3	3	4	5	6	7	8	9	10	11	12
4	4	5	6	7	8	9	10	11	12	13
5	5	6	7	8	9	10	11	12	13	14
6	6	7	8	9	10	11	12	13	14	15
7	7	8	9	10	11	12	13	14	15	16
8	8	9	10	11	12	13	14	15	16	17
9	9	10	11	12	13	14	15	16	17	18

double bar graph *See* bar graph.

double line graph *See* line graph.

dozen (doz)

A dozen is a set of 12 items.

dry measure

Dry measure is used to measure the volume of items such as fruits, vegetables, and grains.

In the system of dry measure, 2 pints = 1 quart, 8 quarts = 1 peck, and 4 pecks = 1 bushel.

Dry pints and dry quarts are a little larger than liquid pints and liquid quarts.

dry pint

A dry pint is a unit of capacity in the customary system of measurement. It is slightly larger than a liquid pint and is used to measure dry products such as fruits and grains.

dry quart

A dry quart is a unit of capacity in the customary system of measurement. It is slightly larger than a liquid quart and is used to measure dry products such as fruits and grains.

See also dry measure; quart.

edge

An edge is a line segment formed where two faces of a space figure meet.

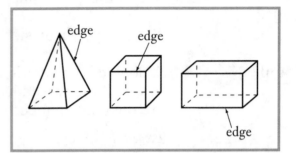

This picture of Monument Valley provides a model for an edge.

elapsed time

Elapsed time is the amount of time that has passed.

element

An element is a member of a set.

Example
The set of whole numbers is {0, 1, 2, 3, 4, 5, 6, . . . }.
4 is an element of the set of whole numbers.

See also set.

ellipse

An ellipse is a special oval shape that resembles a flattened circle.

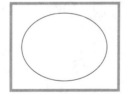

Related word elliptical

Did You Know?

Earth's path around the sun is elliptical (similar to an ellipse).

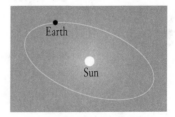

empty set

An empty set is a set with no members.

endpoint

An endpoint is a point at the end of a line segment or ray.

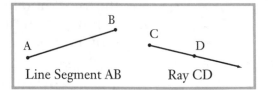

Line Segment AB   Ray CD

Points A and B are endpoints for the line segment.
Point C is the endpoint for the ray.

equal

Equal means "having the same amount, size, or value or being identical."

Examples
There is an equal number of people and chairs.

The pizza is cut into pieces of equal size.

12 inches are equal to 1 foot.

The area of this rectangle is equal to the product of its length and width (A = *l* × *w*).

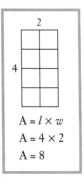

A = *l* × *w*
A = 4 × 2
A = 8

Related words equality, equation, inequality
See also equal sign; equality.

E

equality

Equality is a relationship between two quantities that are of the same amount, size, or value. When an equality is a number relationship, it is expressed by a mathematical sentence that uses the equal sign (=).

Examples
4 + 6 = 10
4 + 6 and 10 name the same number.
$3n = 12$
In this equation, $3n$ and 12 name the same number.

See also equation.

equally likely outcomes

Equally likely outcomes are outcomes that have the same chance of occurring.

See also outcome.

equal ratios

Equal ratios are ratios that describe the same rate or make the same comparison.

Example
Samantha wants to buy and stock an aquarium. She saves $1 of every $5 she earns.

Saved	$1	$2	$3	$4	$5
Earned	$5	$10	$15	$20	$25

1:5, 2:10, 3:15, 4:20, and 5:25 are all equal ratios.

These ratios can also be written as $\frac{1}{5}$, $\frac{2}{10}$, $\frac{3}{15}$, $\frac{4}{20}$, and $\frac{5}{25}$.

See also proportion; ratio.

equal sign (=)

Read as *is equal to* or *equals*. The equal sign (=) indicates that one amount, size, or value is the same as another.

Examples:
2 + 3 = 5   1 hour = 60 minutes $\frac{1}{4} = \frac{2}{8}$

equation

An equation is a mathematical sentence that gives two names for the same number. It is written with an equal sign (=).

variable An equation can have a missing number. The symbol that represents the missing number is called a variable.

Examples
$7 \times \square = 63$ $y \times 8 = 48$

See also variable.

equilateral	*Equilateral* means "having all sides of equal length."

equilateral polygon	Each of these polygons has sides of equal length. They are equilateral polygons.

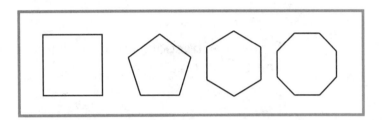

See also equilateral; polygon.

equilateral triangle	This triangle has all sides of equal length. It is an equilateral triangle. *See also* equilateral; triangle.

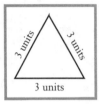

 Did You Know?

The Star of David is a symbol of the Republic of Israel. It is formed by two interlocking equilateral triangles. You can find it on Israel's flag.

equivalent	*Equivalent* means "having the same value."

Examples
5 pennies are equivalent to 1 nickel.
$\frac{4}{4}$ is equivalent to $\frac{2}{2}$ or 1.
4 + 2 and 7 - 1 are equivalent expressions. They name the same number.

equivalent fractions	Equivalent fractions are fractions that name the same number. Also called equal fractions.

Example
These pictures show that $\frac{2}{2} = \frac{4}{4}$.

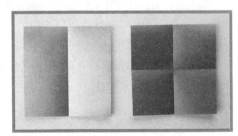

equivalent fractions
(continued)

To name equivalent fractions, multiply the fraction by a fractional name for 1 ($\frac{2}{2}$, $\frac{3}{3}$, $\frac{4}{4}$, $\frac{5}{5}$, . . .).

Examples

$$\frac{1}{2} \times \boxed{\frac{2}{2}} = \frac{2}{4} \qquad\qquad \frac{1}{2} \times \boxed{\frac{3}{3}} = \frac{3}{6} \qquad\qquad \frac{1}{2} \times \boxed{\frac{4}{4}} = \frac{4}{8}$$

Equivalent fractions are used when adding and subtracting unlike fractions.

Examples

$$\frac{1}{2} + \frac{1}{3} = \boxed{}$$

<u>First:</u> Think, what is a denominator that can be used for both fractions? (Find a common multiple of 3 and 2.)
6 is a common multiple. It can be used as a denominator for both fractions.

<u>Next:</u> Express $\frac{1}{2}$ and $\frac{1}{3}$ as equivalent fractions that have a denominator of 6.

$$\frac{1}{2} \times \boxed{\frac{3}{3}} = \frac{3}{6} \qquad\qquad \frac{1}{3} \times \boxed{\frac{2}{2}} = \frac{2}{6} \qquad\qquad \frac{3}{6} + \frac{2}{6} = \frac{5}{6}$$

estimate

An estimate is a number close to an exact number. It is used when an exact number is not needed.
To estimate is to find such a number.

Related word estimation

See also estimation strategies.

estimation strategies

Estimation strategies are ways used to find a number that is close enough to an exact number for our purposes.

amounts Often we want to estimate how much or how many there are. In these cases the use of a benchmark is a helpful strategy. (A benchmark is a reference point that can be used to help in making an estimate.)

Example
<u>Question:</u> Do we have enough milk for 4 people to have cereal? (We usually use a little less than a quart of milk.)
<u>Benchmark:</u> We know that 1 quart = $\frac{1}{4}$ gallon. If the container is filled about $\frac{1}{4}$ of the way, it contains about 1 quart.

<u>Answer:</u> The gallon container of milk is more than $\frac{1}{4}$ full, so there is plenty for breakfast cereal.

computational estimation   We use computational estimation when we want to predict what the result of an operation would be. We do not need to do the computation to get an exact answer when an approximate number is close enough for our purposes.

Five major strategies for computational estimation are clustering, compatible numbers, front-end estimation, rounding, and finding a range.

clustering   Clustering is a method used for estimating a result when numbers appear to group, or cluster, around a common number.

Example
Kathy sold 32 boxes of Girl Scout cookies on Monday, 25 boxes on Tuesday, and 36 boxes on Wednesday.

About how many boxes of cookies did she sell in three days?
32, 25, and 36 cluster around 30.
$3 \times 30 = 90$
Kathy sold about 90 boxes of cookies in three days.

compatible numbers   Compatible numbers are numbers that seem to "go together." They are easy to compute mentally.

Example
Robert bought 3 pencils for $.79. How much did he pay for each pencil?

$.79 is close to $.75, a number compatible with 3.
(Three quarters are equal to $.75).
Robert paid a little more than a quarter ($.25) for each pencil.

front-end estimation   Front-end estimation is a strategy for estimating a result by using the first digit at the front of numbers, followed by zeros, in computing.

Example
Brent and his friends went to the ice-cream shop after the ballgame. They bought 5 milkshakes for $1.19 each.

About how much did they spend?
Front-end $1.19 to $1.00.
$5 \times \$1.00 = \$5.00$
Brent and his friends spent about $5.00 for milkshakes.

estimation strategies
(continued)

rounding Rounding strategies are sometimes used in computational estimation. Rounding a whole number results in a number close to the original number. It usually has the same number of digits, but more of them are zeros.

Example
Salita's mother commutes from New York to Washington, D.C. once each week. The round-trip flight is about 370 miles.

About how many miles does she commute each month?
370, rounded to the nearest 100, is 400.
There are about 4 weeks in a month.
$4 \times 400 = 1600$
Salita's mother commutes about 1600 miles each month.

finding a range Finding a range also uses rounding for computational estimation. The numbers being used are rounded up to make an estimate. This estimate gives the upper end of the range within which the exact answer falls. The numbers being used are also rounded down to make an estimate. This estimate gives the lower end of the range within which the exact answer falls. The exact answer will fall within the range between the two estimates.

Example
Tammy and Clinton were camping in Yellowstone National Park. They wanted to travel south to Jackson, Wyoming, and then on to Bear Lake State Park, in Utah.
About how many miles did they need to travel?

Yellowstone to Jackson	98 miles
Jackson to Bear Lake State Park	146 miles

Estimate 1
98, rounded up, is 100.
146, rounded up, is 150.
$100 + 150 = 250$
250 is the upper end of the range.

Estimate 2
98, rounded down, is 90.
146, rounded down, is 140.

| estimation strategies (continued) | $90 + 140 = 230$
230 is the lower end of the range.
98 + 146 is in the range between 230 and 250.
Tammy and Clinton need to travel between 230 and 250 miles to get to Bear Lake State Park. |

See also clustering; compatible numbers; front-end estimation; range; rounding.

even number

An even number is a whole number that can be divided by two with no remainder.

Example
Even numbers have 0, 2, 4, 6, or 8 in the ones place.

Did You Know?

Gloves, socks, and shoes are packaged in even numbers. So are most other items that have more than one per package.

event

An event is one or more outcomes of an experiment.

Example
If you roll a die, some of the events include rolling a number greater than 4, rolling a 6, rolling a number less than or equal to 3, and rolling a 4.

expanded form

The expanded form of a number is that number written in a way that shows the value of each of its digits. Also called expanded notation. When exponents are used, also called exponential notation.

There are several ways to write a number in expanded form.

Examples for 423:
$400 + 20 + 3$
$(4 \times 100) + (2 \times 10) + (3 \times 1)$
$(4 \times 10^2) + (2 \times 10^1) + (3 \times 10^0)$

E

experiment

In probability an experiment is any activity that has two or more possible results or outcomes. Some simple probability experiments include tossing a coin, rolling a die, and checking to see if it is raining outside.

exponent

An exponent is a number that tells how many times the base is used as a factor.

Example
In 5^3, 5 is the base and 3 is the exponent.
($5^3 = 5 \times 5 \times 5 = 125$)

expression

An expression is a mathematical phrase without an equal sign.

Examples
If one pair of shoes costs $19.99, how can the cost of 4 pairs of shoes at the same price be expressed?
$4 \times 19.99 is an expression for the cost of 4 pairs of shoes.

In algebra, expressions include variables.

$3 + x$ is an expression that means 3 plus a number.
$5n$ is an expression that means the product of 5 and a number.
$\frac{y}{2}$ means a number divided by 2.

face

A face is a side of a space figure formed by polygons.

polyhedron A space figure with polygons for faces is a polyhedron.

Example
This rectangular pyramid has five faces. Four faces are triangles and one face, also called the base, is a rectangle.

See also polyhedron.

fact family

A fact family is formed by related addition and subtraction facts or by related multiplication and division facts. Also called related facts and related sentences.

addition and subtraction fact family An addition and subtraction fact family uses two addends and their sum to form basic facts.

Examples
Fact family using 3, 4, and 7
$$3 + 4 = 7$$
$$4 + 3 = 7$$
$$7 - 4 = 3$$
$$7 - 3 = 4$$

Fact family using 8, 0, and 8
$$8 + 0 = 8$$
$$0 + 8 = 8$$
$$8 - 0 = 8$$
$$8 - 8 = 0$$

multiplication and division fact family A multiplication and division fact family uses two factors and their product to form basic facts.

Example
Fact family using 4, 6, and 24
$$4 \times 6 = 24$$
$$6 \times 4 = 24$$
$$24 \div 6 = 4$$
$$24 \div 4 = 6$$

Fact family using 5, 0, and 0
$$5 \times 0 = 0$$
$$0 \times 5 = 0$$
$$0 \div 5 = 0$$
(There is no fourth member of this fact family. $5 \div 0$ is undefined.)

See also basic facts.

factor

A factor is any of the numbers multiplied to form a product.

Example
In the multiplication sentence $4 \times 3 = 12$, 4 and 3 are factors and 12 is the product. Both 4 and 3 divide 12. That is, $12 \div 4 = 3$ with no remainder, and $12 \div 3 = 4$ with no remainder.

factors of a number The factors of a number are all the numbers that divide that number.

Example
The whole number factors of 12 are 1, 2, 3, 4, 6, and 12.

factoring Factoring is the process of writing a number or expression as the product of its factors.

See also common factor; factor pair; factor tree; greatest common factor; prime factor; prime factorization; proper factor.

factor pair

A factor pair is a set of two numbers that, when multiplied, will result in a given product.

Example
In $2 \times 6 = 12$, the factor pair for 12 is (2, 6).
Other factor pairs for 12 include (1, 12) and (3, 4).

factor tree

A factor tree is a diagram showing factors of a number, ending when the prime factors of that number have been found. Different factor trees may be used for the same number, but the prime factorization is the same.

Example

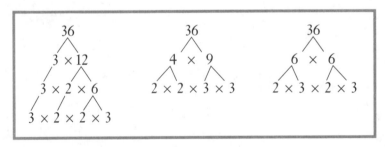

The prime factorization of 36 is $2 \times 2 \times 3 \times 3$ (or $2^2 \times 3^2$).

See also prime factor; prime factorization.

Fahrenheit (°F) temperature scale

The Fahrenheit (°F) temperature scale is used for measuring temperature in the customary system. Also called Fahrenheit scale.

Tools of the Trade

Two reference points for this temperature scale are:

32°   the freezing point of water
212° the boiling point of water

Water Boils 212°

Water freezes 32°

Did You Know?

The Fahrenheit temperature scale was developed in the early 1700s by a German scientist named Gabriel David Fahrenheit. He was the first person to make a mercury thermometer.

See also Celsius (°C) temperature scale; temperature.

fathom

A fathom is a unit of length equal to 6 feet. It is used for measuring the depth of water

favorable outcome

A favorable outcome is a result that meets the condition being investigated in an experiment.

Example
If a coin is tossed to see how likely it is to land heads up, landing on its tail is a favorable outcome.

See also outcome.

figurate numbers

Figurate numbers are numbers that can be represented by arrays that look like various plane figures. Also called polygonal numbers.

See also pentagonal numbers; polygonal numbers; square numbers; triangular numbers.

flip

A flip is a mirror image of a figure. Also called reflection.

See also slide; turn.

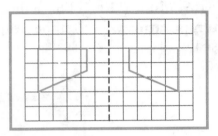

fluid ounce (fl oz)

A fluid ounce is a unit of capacity in the customary system of measurement.
8 fluid ounces = 1 cup

See also capacity; customary system of measurement; ounce.

foot

pl. **feet** A foot is a unit of length in the customary system of measurement.
1 foot = 12 inches

See also customary system of measurement.

formula

A formula is an equation that expresses a mathematical relationship, principle, or rule.

Example
Jessica and her family were planning a long road trip. They planned to travel 8 hours a day by car, averaging about 55 miles each hour. What is the distance they could travel each day?

This problem can be solved using the following formula.
$D = R \times T$ (Distance is equal to the Rate of travel times the Time traveled.)
$D = 55 \times 8$
$D = 440$, the number of miles that Jessica's family could travel each day.

fraction

A fraction is a number that can be expressed as $\frac{a}{b}$, in which *a* and *b* are any number and *b* is not equal to zero. *Fraction* is used to mean "fractional number." It is also used as a shortened form of the term *common fraction*.

See also common fraction; fractional number.

fractional number

A fractional number is used to express a part of a whole or a group. A fractional number may also be used to express a ratio.

fractional number
(continued)

A fractional number may be written in three different ways: as a common fraction, a decimal fraction, or a percent.

Examples

$\frac{1}{2}$, 0.5, or 50% of this circle is shaded.

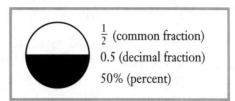

$\frac{1}{2}$ (common fraction)
0.5 (decimal fraction)
50% (percent)

$\frac{1}{2}$, 0.5, or 50% of these squares are shaded.

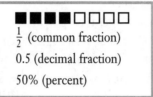

$\frac{1}{2}$ (common fraction)
0.5 (decimal fraction)
50% (percent)

$\frac{1}{2}$, 0.5, and 50% are all names for the same fractional number.

See also common fraction; decimal fraction; percent.

fraction bar

A fraction bar is a horizontal bar that separates the numerator and the denominator of a common fraction. The numerator is written above the fraction bar. The denominator is written below the fraction bar.

$$\frac{1}{2} \longleftarrow \text{fraction bar}$$

frequency

Frequency is the number of times an item occurs in a set of data.

frequency table

A frequency table is used to summarize the number of times items occur in a set of data. Tally marks are often used to record the frequency of an item. Also called tally chart.

How We Get to School	
Walk	卌 |||
Ride a bus	||||
Ride in a car	||
Ride a bicycle	卌 卌	

front-end digit

The front-end digit in a number is the first digit, reading the number from left to right. It is the digit in the number that has the greatest place value.

See also front-end estimation.

F

front-end estimation

Front-end estimation is a strategy for estimating sums, differences, products, or quotients by using front-end digits followed by zeros.

To do front-end estimation, keep the first digit at the front of each number to be used (the front-end digit). Use zeros in place of the remaining digits. Then add, subtract, multiply, or divide mentally.

Example
In 1996 the population of Mexico City, Mexico, was recorded as 8,235,744. An additional 6,811,941 people lived in the surrounding area. About how many people lived in Mexico City and the surrounding area?
8,235,744 $\longrightarrow$ 8,000,000   6,811,941 $\longrightarrow$ 6,000,000
8,000,000 + 6,000,000 = 14,000,000
More than 14,000,000 people lived in Mexico City and the surrounding area in 1996.

See also estimation strategies.

ft²

Read as *square foot*. A ft² is the amount of area enclosed by a square that measures 1 foot by 1 foot. Also written as square foot and sq ft.

See also square unit.

ft³

Read as *cubic foot*. A ft³ is equal to the volume of a cube that measures 1 foot on each edge. Also written as cubic foot.

See also cubic unit.

function

A function is a relation between two sets in which each member of the first set is paired with one and only one member of the second set. Two of the ways that functions may be shown are by mapping and by using tables. Also called mapping.

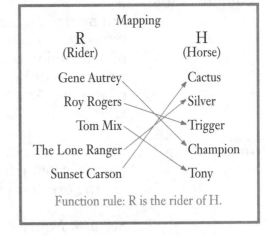

Mapping

R
(Rider)

H
(Horse)

Gene Autrey   Cactus
Roy Rogers   Silver
Tom Mix   Trigger
The Lone Ranger   Champion
Sunset Carson   Tony

Function rule: R is the rider of H.

function
(continued)

Function Table

A	B
0	0
12	3
28	7
36	9
32	8
24	6
8	2
20	5
4	1
16	4

Function rule: A is the product of B and 4.

function rule   A function rule is a rule that explains the relationship between two sets.

furlong   A furlong is a unit of length equal to $\frac{1}{8}$ mile. It is used to measure distances of horse races.

 Did You Know?

The Kentucky Derby, the world's most famous horse race, is held on the first Saturday of May each year at the Churchill Downs in Louisville, KY. It is a 10-furlong (1 $\frac{1}{4}$ mile) race for three-year-old horses.

gallon (gal)

A gallon is a unit of capacity in the customary system of measurement.

1 gallon = 4 quarts

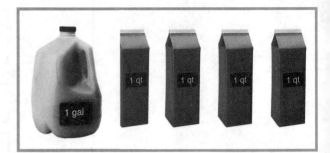

Did You Know?

A half-gallon carton of ice cream will serve 8 people each a cup of ice cream.

See also capacity; customary system of measurement.

GCF (greatest common factor)

The GCF is the largest factor that two or more numbers share.

See also greatest common factor.

geobands

Geobands are rubber bands used for constructing geometric figures on geoboards.

See also geoboard.

geoboard

A geoboard is a board with regularly spaced pegs that is used for exploring plane figures.

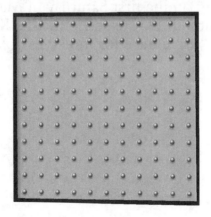

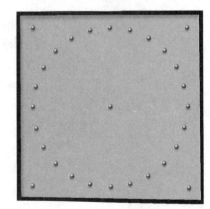

geometric figure

A geometric figure is any combination of points, lines, or planes. Also called geometric shape.

space figure A space figure is a three-dimensional geometric figure, or a figure that occupies space and has volume.

Example
This tent is in the shape of a space figure, a triangular prism.

This drawing shows the three dimensions of a triangular prism.

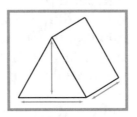

plane figure A plane figure is a two-dimensional geometric figure. It has no thickness and lies entirely in one plane.

Example
This triangular prism has plane figures for faces. Two of the faces are triangles.

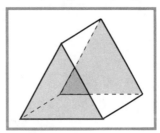

lines, line segments, and rays Lines, line segments, and rays are one-dimensional geometric figures.

Example
The base of this triangle is a line segment. It has one dimension—length.

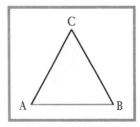

points Look at the triangle above and locate points A, B, and C. These points could be called zero-dimensional geometric figures because they do not occupy space.

See also line; line segment; one-dimensional; plane figure; point; ray; space figure; three-dimensional; two-dimensional; zero-dimensional.

geometry

Geometry is the branch of mathematics that includes the study of shape, size, and other properties of figures. It is one of the oldest branches of mathematics, probably used even in prehistoric times.

Did You Know?

The kind of geometry most students usually study was recorded in *The Elements*, a set of books written about 300 B.C. by Euclid, a Greek mathematician. There are now other kinds of geometry. These other kinds originated about 2000 years after Euclid's work.

Related word geometric

Golden rectangle

A Golden rectangle is a rectangle for which the ratio of length to width is approximately 8 to 5.

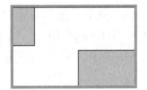

See also rectangle.

googol

A googol is a number equal to 1 followed by 100 zeros, or 10^{100}.

Did You Know?

Edward Kasner, an American mathematician, was working with 10^{100}. He asked his nephew what he might call it. His nephew named it googol.

Related word googolplex

gram (g)

A gram is a unit of weight in the metric system of measurement.

1000 grams = 1 kilogram

See also metric system of measurement.

graph

A graph is a kind of drawing that shows mathematical information, ideas, and relationships. In statistics, examples of graphs used to represent data are bar graphs, picture graphs, circle graphs, line graphs, line plots, and stem-and-leaf plots.

In algebra and geometry, number lines are used to graph numbers. The coordinate system is used to graph ordered pairs, equations, and other mathematical relationships.

See also bar graph; circle graph; coordinate system; double bar graph; line graph; line plot; picture graph; real graph; stem-and-leaf plot.

graph scale

Graph scale is the ratio between the picture, or icon, on a graph and the number it represents.

See also graph; scale.

greater than or equal to sign ($\geq$)

Read as *is greater than or equal to.* The greater than or equal to sign ($\geq$) is used to compare two numbers when the first number expressed is greater than or equal to the second number.

Examples

7 ($\geq$) 4	Read as Seven is greater than or equal to four.
3 × 4 ($\geq$) 2 × 5	Read as Three times four is greater than or equal to two times five.

See also inequality.

greater than sign (>)

Read as *is greater than.* The greater than sign (>) is used to compare two numbers when the greater number is expressed first.

Examples

8 >7	Read as Eight is greater than seven.
2 × 3 > 2 × 2	Read as Two times three is greater than two times two.

See also inequality.

greatest common factor (GCF)

The greatest common factor (GCF) is the largest factor shared by two or more numbers. The greatest common factor for two or more numbers may be found by listing factors or by using prime factorization. Also called greatest common divisor.

greatest common factor (continued)

listing factors For smaller numbers, listing factors is usually not too hard to do and is helpful in finding the greatest common factor.

Example
To find the greatest common factor of 8 and 12, first list the factors.

Factors of 8 are   1, 2, 4, 8.
Factors of 12 are   1, 2, 3, 4, 6, 12.

Next, look at these factors and see which is the largest factor that the two numbers share.
The greatest common factor of 8 and 12 is 4.
This can also be written as GCF (8, 12) = 4.

using prime factorization For larger numbers, listing factors is usually more difficult. In these cases, prime factorization is helpful.

Example
To find the greatest common factor of 36 and 48, first find the prime factorization.

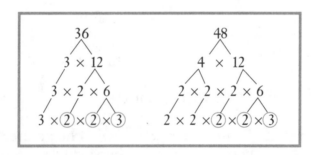

The numbers 36 and 48 have the prime factors 2, 2, and 3 in common.
Multiply these prime factors: $2 \times 2 \times 3 = 12$.
GCF (36, 48) = 12
Knowing how to find the greatest common factor is helpful in expressing common fractions in their simplest form.

See also common factor; simplest form.

grid

A grid is a set of uniformly spaced horizontal and vertical lines.

See also coordinate system.

gross

A gross is equal to 12 dozens (12 × 12), or 144. Gross also is the total before any deductions.

Did You Know?

School pencils are often ordered by the gross. There are 12 pencils in each package, and 12 packages in each box of pencils

gross income

Gross income is the total amount of money earned before taxes and other items are deducted.

grouping property

The grouping property means that changing the grouping of the numbers used in an operation without changing the order does not change the result of that operation. Also called associative property.

See also associative property.

grouping property of addition

The grouping property of addition means that when adding three or more numbers, we can group the numbers in any way we choose without changing the order and the sum will remain the same. Also called associative property of addition.

See also associative property of addition.

grouping property of multiplication

The grouping property of multiplication means that when multiplying three or more numbers, we can group the numbers in any way we choose without changing the order and the product will remain the same. Also called associative property of multiplication.

See also associative property of multiplication.

hecto-

Hecto- is a prefix meaning " hundred."

Examples
1 hectometer = 100 meters   1 hectoliter = 100 liters
1 hectogram = 100 grams

See also metric system of measurement.

hectogram (hg)

A hectogram is a unit of weight in the metric system of measurement.
1 hectogram = 100 grams

See also metric system of measurement.

hectoliter (hL)

A hectoliter is a unit of capacity in the metric system of measurement.
1 hectoliter = 100 liters

See also metric system of measurement.

hectometer (hm)

A hectometer is a unit of length in the metric system of measurement.
1 hectometer = 100 meters

 Did You Know?

The Statue of Liberty, one of the world's tallest statues, measures about 93 meters from its foundation to the top of the torch. This distance is nearly one hectometer.

See also metric system of measurement.

height

The height of a geometric figure is its altitude. Height also refers to how tall somebody or something is.

Example
The tallest animal is the giraffe. It grows to a height of about 5.5 meters. The tallest living thing is believed to be a redwood tree, reaching a height of about 105 meters.

See also altitude.

hemisphere

A hemisphere is half of a sphere. (*Hemi-* means "half.") Earth can be divided into the Northern Hemisphere and the Southern Hemisphere. Earth can also be divided into the Eastern Hemisphere and the Western Hemisphere.

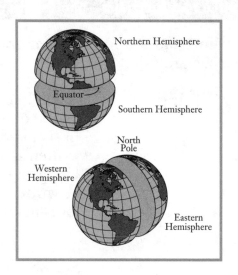

heptagon

A heptagon is a polygon with 7 sides. (*Hepta-* means "seven.")

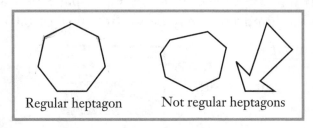

Regular heptagon Not regular heptagons

See also polygon.

hexagon

A hexagon is a polygon with 6 sides. (*Hexa-* means "six.")

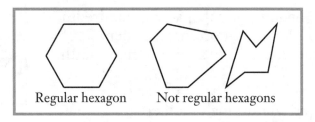

Regular hexagon Not regular hexagons

See also polygon.

Hindu-Arabic numeration system

The Hindu-Arabic numeration system is a base-ten system of numeration in which the digits 0, 1, 2, 3, 4, 5, 6, 7, 8, and 9 are used.

See also decimal numeration system.

horizontal axis

The horizontal axis is the horizontal number line in a rectangular coordinate system. Also called x-axis.

See also coordinate system.

horizontal bar graph	*See* bar graph.

hundred

A hundred is equal to 10 tens or 100 ones.
In standard form a hundred is written as 100.
Using an exponent, 100 may be written as 1×10^2 (or simply as 10^2).

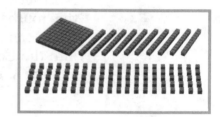

See also decimal numeration system.

hundredth

A hundredth is one of 100 equal parts of a whole or a group. One hundredth may be written as $\frac{1}{100}$ or 0.01.

Examples
A penny or cent is one hundredth of a dollar.

The unit, or cube, is one hundredth of the flat. In ordinal numbers, hundredth is next after ninety-ninth.

See also ordinal number.

hundredths

In the decimal numeration system, hundredths is the name of the next place to the right of tenths. In the number 2.98, the 8 is in the hundredths place.

ones	.	tenths	hundredths
2	.	9	8

See also decimal numeration system; hundredth.

icosahedron

An icosahedron is a space figure with 20 faces.

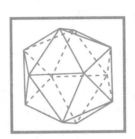 

See also polyhedron.

identity element

An identity element is a number that when used in an operation with another number leaves that number the same. The identity element for addition is 0. When 0 is added to any number, that number remains the same, or keeps its identity.

Example
4 + 0 = 0 + 4 = 4

The identity element for multiplication is 1. When 1 is multiplied by any number, that number remains the same, or keeps its identity.

Example
4 × 1 = 1 × 4 = 4

See also identity property for addition; identity property for multiplication.

identity property for addition

The identity property for addition means that the sum of 0 and any number is that number. Also called identity property of 0 for addition and zero property of addition.

Example
27 + 0 = 0 + 27 = 27
The identity property for addition may be written with symbols as $a + 0 = 0 + a = a$.

See also identity element; identity property for multiplication.

identity property for multiplication

The identity property for multiplication means that the product of 1 and any number is that number. Also called identity property of 1 for multiplication.

Example
$8 \times 1 = 1 \times 8 = 8$
The identity property for multiplication may be written with symbols as $a \times 1 = 1 \times a = a$

See also identity element; identity property for addition.

improper fraction

An improper fraction is a common fraction that names a number equal to or greater than 1.

Examples
$\frac{3}{2}$ $\frac{8}{4}$ $\frac{19}{6}$ $\frac{4}{4}$ $\frac{100}{75}$

For each improper fraction, the numerator is equal to or greater than the denominator.

See also common fraction; proper fraction.

in.²

Read as *square inch*. A in.² is the amount of area enclosed by a square that measures 1 inch by 1 inch. Also written as square inch and sq in.

See also square unit.

in.³

Read as *cubic inch*. A in.³ is equal to the volume of a cube that measures 1 inch on each edge. Also written as cubic inch.

See also cubic unit.

inch (in.)

An inch is a unit of length in the customary system of measurement.   12 inches = 1 foot

Did You Know?

At one time in English history, an inch was defined as the width of a man's thumb. Today an inch is defined as 2.54 cm, which is about the length of a child's thumb from the tip to the first joint.

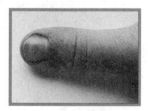

See also customary system of measurement.

independent events	Independent events are events that have no effect on each other.

inequality

An inequality is a relationship between two different quantities. An inequality may be expressed by a mathematical sentence that uses one of the following symbols.

< (is less than)

> (is greater than)

≤ (is less than or equal to)

≥ (is greater than or equal to)

≠ (is not equal to)

Examples

$\frac{1}{2} < \frac{3}{4}$

$99.8 > 98.6$

$3 \times 2 \leq 4 + 3$

$11 \geq 9$

$2 + 3 \neq 2 \times 3$

See also equality; equal sign (=); greater than or equal to sign (≥); greater than sign (>); less than or equal to sign (≤); less than sign (<); not equal to sign (≠).

infinite

Infinite means "unending."

Example

The set of even numbers is infinite: 2, 4, 6, 8, 10, 12, . . .

The three dots (. . .) are used to show that the set is unending.

Related word infinity

integers

Integers are the counting numbers, their opposites, and zero.

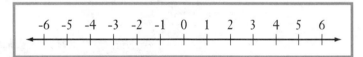

positive integers Positive integers are integers greater than 0.

negative integers Negative integers are integers less than 0. 0 is neither positive nor negative.

interest

Interest is the charge for borrowing money or the amount paid for money invested.

simple interest To find simple interest, multiply the amount of money (principal) by the percent (rate) by the number of years (time).
Expressed as a formula:

Interest = principal × rate × time

or $I = p \times r \times t$

Example
Becky borrowed $20 from her mother for six months at 6% interest. How much did she owe her mother at the end of six months?

$I = p \times r \times t$
p (principal) = $20
r (rate) = 6%, or 0.06
t (time) = 6 months, or $\frac{1}{2}$ year
$I = \$20 \times 0.06 \times \frac{1}{2} = \$.60$

At the end of six months, Becky owed her mother the principal, $20, plus the interest, $.60, for a total of $20.60.

See also principal; rate.

intersect

Intersect means "to meet, cross, or overlap."

lines, rays, line segments, and planes For lines, rays, line segments, and planes, intersect means "to meet or cross." When two lines, rays, or line segments intersect, they have one common point.

Examples
These streets represent lines that intersect, or cross, at this intersection.

intersect
(continued)

Point (3, 4) is the intersection of line $x = 3$ and line $y = 4$. When two planes intersect, they meet at a line.

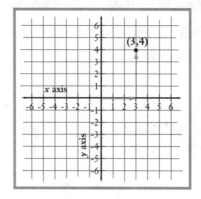

other geometric figures For other geometric figures, intersect means "to overlap or cross at more than one point."

This sculpture shows intersecting planes.

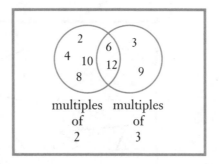

Sets may also intersect, or share common elements. This Venn diagram shows the intersection of multiples of 2 and 3 within the set of whole numbers from 1–12.

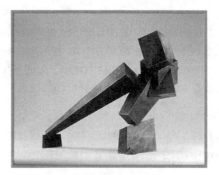

See also parallel lines; parallel planes.

intersecting lines

Intersecting lines are lines that cross at one point.

See also intersect.

intersecting planes

Intersecting planes are planes that meet at a line.

See also intersect.

inverse operations

Inverse operations are two operations, in which one "undoes" the other. Addition and subtraction are inverse operations. Multiplication and division are also inverse operations. Also called opposite operations.

See also opposite operations.

irrational number

An irrational number is a number that cannot be written in the form of a common fraction. When an irrational number is written in decimal form, it is written with three dots (. . .) to show that it does not end.

Example
3.14159. . . (a value for π) is an irrational number. It is unending and nonrepeating.

See also nonterminating decimal.

irregular polygon

An irregular polygon has sides and angles that are not congruent.

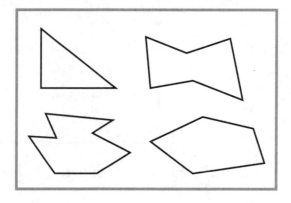

See also polygon.

isosceles trapezoid

An isosceles trapezoid is a trapezoid with its nonparallel sides the same length.

See also trapezoid.

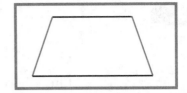

isosceles triangle

An isosceles triangle is a triangle that has two sides of equal length.

See also triangle.

key

The key of a map or a graph is the part that explains the symbols. Also called legend.

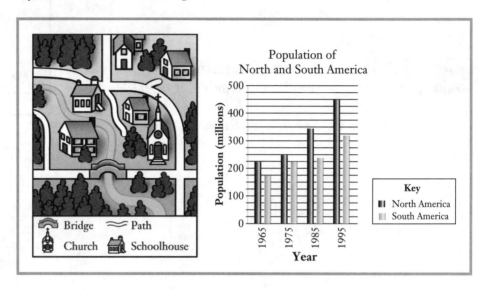

kilo-

Kilo- is a prefix meaning "thousand."

Examples
1 kilometer = 1000 meters
1 kiloliter = 1000 liters
1 kilogram = 1000 grams

See also metric system of measurement.

kilogram (kg)

A kilogram is a unit of weight in the metric system of measurement.
1 kilogram = 1000 grams

kiloliter (kL)

A kiloliter is a unit of capacity in the metric system of measurement.
1 kiloliter = 1000 liters

Example
A cube that measures 1 meter on each edge has a capacity of 1 kiloliter. A kiloliter of water weighs a metric ton.

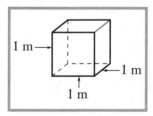

kilometer (km)   A kilometer is a unit of length in the metric system of measurement.
1 kilometer = 1000 meters

kite   A kite is a quadrilateral with two pairs of sides that are of equal length. These equal sides are next to each other. No two sides are parallel.

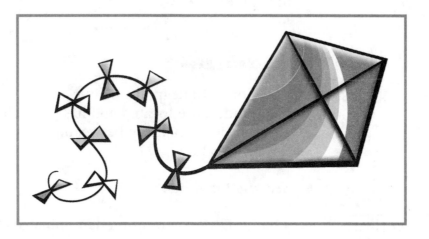

See also quadrilateral.

km²   Read as square kilometer. A km² is equal to the area enclosed by a square that measures 1 kilometer by 1 kilometer.

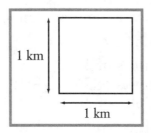

Large land and water areas are measured in km².

 Did You Know?

The area of 25 city blocks is about 1 km².
The Pacific Ocean, the largest ocean on Earth, has a surface area of about 165,250,000 km².

See also square unit.

83

L

latitude

Latitude is a distance north or south of the equator. This distance is measured in degrees.

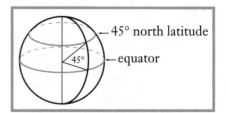

Both Minneapolis, Minnesota (USA), and Bordeaux, France, are located about 45° north latitude. This latitude is halfway between the equator and the North Pole.

See also longitude.

LCD (least common denominator)

The LCD (least common denominator) for two or more fractions is the least common multiple of the denominators other than 0.

Examples
What is the least common denominator of $\frac{1}{4}$ and $\frac{1}{6}$?
Multiples of 4:   4, 8, 12, . . .
Multiples of 6:   6, 12, . . .
The least common denominator of $\frac{1}{4}$ and $\frac{1}{6}$ is 12.

What is the LCD of $\frac{3}{4}$, $\frac{2}{5}$, and $\frac{1}{2}$?
Multiples of 4:   4, 8, 12, 16, 20, . . .
Multiples of 5:   5, 10, 15, 20, . . .
Multiples of 2:   2, 4, 6, 8, 10, 12, 14, 16, 18, 20, . . .
The least common denominator of $\frac{3}{4}$, $\frac{2}{5}$, and $\frac{1}{2}$ is 20.

See also common multiple.

LCM (least common multiple)

The least common multiple (LCM) of two or more numbers is the smallest nonzero whole number that is a multiple of each number.

Examples
The least common multiple of 2 and 4 is 4.
The least common multiple of 2 and 5 is 10.
The least common multiple of 3, 4, and 6 is 12.

LCM
(least common multiple)
continued

Listing multiples is one way to find the LCM.

Example
To find the LCM of 2, 6, and 9, list the nonzero multiples of each number until you find one that is common to all three numbers.
2, 4, 6, 8, 10, 12, 14, 16, 18, . . .
6, 12, 18, . . .
9, 18, . . .
The LCM of 2, 6, and 9 is 18.
This is written as LCM (2, 6, 9) = 18.

Prime factorization is another way to find the LCM.

Example
To find the LCM of 4 and 6,
first write the prime factorization of each number.
4 = 2 × 2
6 = 2 × 3
Then list the prime factors of both numbers together. Include each prime factor as many times as it appears in 4 or 6.

This Venn diagram will help you see how many times to include each factor in your list of prime factors.

2 × 2 × 3 = 12
LCM (4, 6) = 12

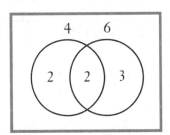

See also common multiple; LCD (least common denominator); multiple.

length

Length usually refers to the measure of the distance from one end of any object or space to the other.

 Did You Know?

A boa constrictor can grow to a length of 10 to 15 feet.

See also customary system of measurement; metric system of measurement.

less than (<)	Read as *is less than*. The symbol for less than (<) is used to compare two unequal numbers when the lesser number is written first. *Examples* $7 < 10$ — Read as Seven is less than ten. $\frac{1}{3} < \frac{1}{2}$ — Read as One third is less than one half. $^-5 < ^-3$ — Read as Negative five is less than negative three. ***See also*** equality; inequality.
less than or equal to (≤)	Read as *is less than or equal to*. The symbol for less than or equal to (≤) is used to compare two numbers when the first number is less than or equal to the second number. *Examples* $5 \le 10$ — Read as Five is less than or equal to ten. $6 \le 6$ — Read as Six is less than or equal to six. ***See also*** equality; inequality.
light-year	A light-year is the distance light travels in one year through space. A light-year is almost six trillion (6,000,000,000,000) miles.
like fractions	Like fractions are fractions with the same denominator. Also called similar fractions. ***See also*** unlike fractions.
line	A line is a collection of points along a straight path extending infinitely in both directions.

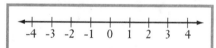

linear measure	Linear measure is the measurement of length. ***See also*** length.
line graph	A line graph is a graph using a broken line to show change. This change usually happens over a period of time.

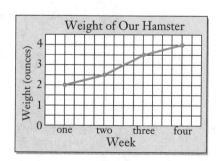

line graph
(continued)

double line graph A double line graph is a set of two graphs shown on the same grid. Double line graphs help in comparing two sets of information.

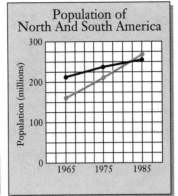

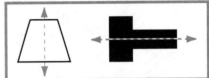

See also double line graph.

line of symmetry

A line of symmetry is a line that divides a figure into two congruent parts. These parts are mirror images. Some figures have more than one line of symmetry.

All the lines of symmetry for the square and triangle are shown. For the circle, only four of an infinite number of lines of symmetry are shown.

See also symmetry.

line plot

A line plot is a graph that shows each item of information on a number line. It can serve as a rough draft of a graph. It has the shape of a bar graph.

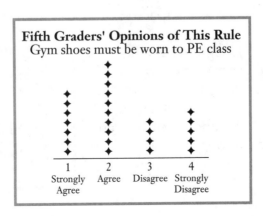

line segment

A line segment is a part of a line having two endpoints.

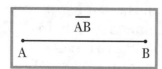

$\overline{AB}$

A   B

line symmetry

A plane figure has line symmetry if it can be divided into two congruent parts that are mirror images. Also called reflectional symmetry.

See also symmetry.

liquid measure

Liquid measure is a measure of capacity, or the amount of liquid a container will hold. Liquid measure usually refers to units in the customary system. These units include cup, pint, quart, and gallon. Some units in the metric system are also used for liquid measure. These units include milliliter and liter.

See also capacity; dry measure.

liter (L)

Liter is the basic unit of capacity in the metric system of measurement.
1 liter = 1000 milliliters

Did You Know?

A liter of water weighs 1 kilogram.
Soda can be bought in 2-liter bottles.
A 2-liter bottle of soda weighs about 2 kilograms.

See also capacity; metric system of measurement.

longitude

Longitude is a distance east or west of an imaginary line on Earth's surface. This distance is measured in degrees.

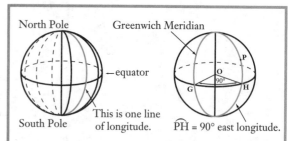

North Pole   Greenwich Meridian

—equator

South Pole   This is one line
               of longitude.

$\overset{\frown}{PH}$ = 90° east longitude.

L

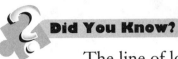
The line of longitude that passes through Greenwich, England, was chosen as 0° longitude because the Royal Greenwich Observatory was located there.

See also latitude.

loss

In business transactions, loss is the difference in expenses and income when expenses are greater than income.

Example
Pedro made some crafts to sell at the craft fair. He paid $15.43 for supplies. He sold all the crafts he made for only $12.00. Not counting the time he spent making the crafts or the additional supplies he borrowed from his mother, what was Pedro's loss?

Pedro's expenses were $15.43.
Pedro's income was $12.00.
15.43 - 12.00 = 3.43
Pedro's loss was $3.43.

See also profit.

lowest terms

A common fraction is in lowest terms if the numerator and denominator have no common factor other than 1. Also called lowest terms of a fraction.

See also simplest form.

L

m²

Read as *square meter*. A m² is equal to the amount of area enclosed by a square that measures 1 meter by 1 meter.

See also square unit.

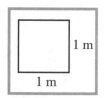

m³

Read as *cubic meter*. A m³ is equal to the volume of a cube that measures 1 meter (100 cm or 10 dm) on each edge. Also written as cubic meter.

See also cubic unit.

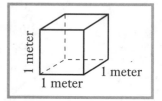

mapping

A mapping is a function, or a relation between two sets in which each member of the first set is paired with one and only one member of the second set. Mapping is also a way to show a function.

See also function.

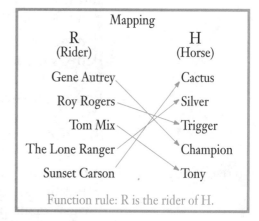

Mapping

R (Rider)   H (Horse)

Gene Autrey   Cactus
Roy Rogers   Silver
Tom Mix   Trigger
The Lone Ranger   Champion
Sunset Carson   Tony

Function rule: R is the rider of H.

map scale

A map scale is a ratio between the dimensions on a map and the dimensions of the area represented by the map.

See also scale.

mass

Mass is the amount of matter in an object. It is usually measured in grams and kilograms. The mass of an object remains the same regardless of location.

This astronaut has the same mass, whether on Earth or in space.

See also weight.

mean

The arithmetic mean of a set of numbers is the most common form of average. To find the mean, first find the sum of the set of numbers and then divide by the number of numbers in the set.

Example
Deanna went bowling last evening. She bowled three games. Her scores were
Game 1   130
Game 2   124
Game 3   133
What was the mean (or average) of her scores for the evening?
130 + 124 + 133 = 387
387 ÷ 3 = 129
The mean of Deanna's bowling scores for the evening was 129.

See also average.

measurement

Measurement is comparing an attribute of an object such as length, capacity, or weight to a unit of measure for that attribute. The measurement of the object is also the number resulting from the comparison.

Example

The attribute that is being measured is length. The unit of length is centimeters. The car measures 4 centimeters in length. This measurement, like all other measurements, is approximate. This is because for every unit of measurement, there is always a smaller, more precise unit that could be used.

There are many other kinds of measurement. Some of these are area, time, temperature, and angle measurement.

See also attribute; customary system of measurement; metric system of measurement.

M

median

The median is the middle number for a set of data when the data are arranged in order from least to greatest or greatest to least. To find the median of a set of numbers, arrange the numbers in order and then find the middle number.

Example (when there is a middle number)
Set of numbers (arranged in order): 1, 3, 6, 9, 12
Median: 6

Example (when there is no single middle number)
If there is no single middle number, the median is the arithmetic mean of the two middle numbers.
Set of numbers: 1, 2, 4, 5, 7, 8
$(4 + 5) \div 2 = 4.5$
Median: 4.5

See also average.

mental computation

Mental computation is doing addition, subtraction, multiplication, or division " in one's head" without using paper and pencil or a calculator. There are many strategies for mental computation. A few of them include using basic facts, the front-end approach, and compatible numbers. Also called mental arithmetic, mental math, and mental mathematics.

Example (using basic facts)
A 6-pack of candy bars costs $2.40. How much does each candy bar cost?
$2.40 \div 6 = ?$
One solution strategy is to think
$24 \div 6 = 4$ (using a basic fact)
so $2.40 \div 6 = .40$
Each candy bar costs $.40

Example (front-end approach)
Bob and Joan traveled 313 miles on the first day of their trip and 178 miles on the second day. How many miles did they travel in both days?
$313 + 178 = ?$
One solution strategy is to think
$300 + 100 = 400$
$10 + 70 = 80$
$3 + 8 = 11$
$400 + 80 + 11 = 491$
Bob and Joan traveled 491 miles in both days.

M

mental computation
(continued)

Example (compatible numbers)
The 32 students in Mr. Clark's class surveyed their favorite fast foods. Of these students, 13 listed pizza as their favorite. How many listed some other food?
32 - 13 = ?
One solution strategy is to think 32 is close to 33. 33 and 13 are compatible numbers.
That is 33 - 13 is easy to compute mentally.
33 - 13 = 20
33 is 1 more than 32, so I will need to subtract 1 from 20.
20 - 1 = 19
In Mr. Clark's class, 19 students listed some other fast food besides pizza as a favorite.

See also estimation strategies.

meter (m)

Meter is a unit of length in the metric system of measurement.
1 meter = 100 centimeters

See also metric system of measurement; length.

metric system of measurement

The metric system of measurement is a base-ten system of measurement. It was developed in France in the late 1700s and is the major system of measurement in almost every country. One exception is the United States, where the customary system of measurement is used in most everyday situations. Also called metric measurement system and metric system.

Some of the units of the metric system are shown in the following table.

	Length	Weight	Capacity
Group 1	millimeter centimeter decimeter	milligram centigram decigram	milliliter centiliter deciliter
Base Unit	meter	gram	liter
Group 2	dekameter hectometer kilometer	dekagram hectogram kilogram	dekaliter hectoliter kiloliter

M

metric system of measurement
(continued)

Base units
The base unit for length is meter. The base unit for weight is gram. The base unit for capacity is liter.

Group 1 prefixes
The prefixes in Group 1 are *milli-*, *centi-*, and *deci-*. These prefixes added to words expressing measurement show that the base unit has been divided by some multiple of 10.

1 millimeter = 0.001 meter   1 milliliter = 0.001 liter
1 centimeter = 0.01 meter   1 centiliter = 0.01 liter
1 decimeter = 0.1 meter   1 deciliter = 0.1 liter

1 milligram = 0.001 gram   All the units in Group 1 are
1 centigram = 0.01 gram   smaller than the base unit.
1 decigram = 0.1 gram

Group 2 prefixes
The prefixes in Group 2 are *deka-*, *hecto-*, and *kilo-*. These prefixes show that the base unit has been multiplied by some multiple of 10.

1 dekameter = 10 meters   1 dekaliter = 10 liters
1 hectometer = 100 meters   1 hectoliter = 100 liters
1 kilometer = 1000 meters   1 kiloliter = 1000 liters

1 dekagram = 10 grams   All the units in Group 2 are
1 hectogram = 100 grams   larger than the base unit.
1 kilogram = 1000 grams

See also capacity; Celsius (°C) temperature scale; centigram; centiliter; centimeter; cm²; cubic unit; decigram; deciliter; decimeter; dekagram; dekaliter; dekameter; gram; hectogram; hectoliter; hectometer; kilogram; kiloliter; kilometer; km²; liter; m²; meter; metric ton; milligram; milliliter; millimeter.

metric ton (t)

Metric ton is a unit of weight in the metric system of measurement.
1 metric ton = 1000 kilograms

Did You Know?

The blue whale is the world's largest animal. It may weigh as much as 135 metric tons. Elephants are the largest land animals and the second largest animals in the world. A large male elephant may weigh more than 5 metric tons.

See also metric system of measurement; ton.

mi²

Read as *square mile*. A mi² is equal to the area enclosed by a square that measures 1 mile by 1 mile.

See also square unit.

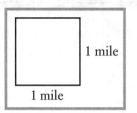

mile (mi)

A mile is a unit of length in the customary system of measurement.
1 mile = 5280 feet or 1760 yards

See also customary system of measurement.

millennium

pl. **millenniums** or **millennia** Millennium is a measure of time.
1 millennium = 1000 years

Did You Know?

The bristlecone pine tree, found in the mountains of Utah and in some other western states, may be the earth's oldest living tree. Several bristlecone pine trees have been found to be more than 4 milleniums old!

milli-

Milli- is a prefix meaning "one thousandth."
1 millimeter = 0.001 meter
1 milliliter = 0.001 liter
1 milligram = 0.001 gram

milligram (mg)

A milligram is a unit of weight in the metric system of measurement.
1000 milligrams = 1 gram

See also metric system of measurement; weight.

milliliter (mL)

A milliliter is a unit of capacity in the metric system of measurement.
1000 milliliters = 1 liter

See also metric system of measurement; capacity.

millimeter (mm)

A millimeter is a unit of length in the metric system of measurement.
1000 millimeters = 1 meter

See also metric system of measurement; length.

million

A million is equal to 1000 thousands. In standard form, one million is written as 1,000,000. With an exponent, one million may be written as 1×10^6 (or simply as 10^6).

See also decimal numeration system.

minute (min)

A minute is a unit for measuring short lengths of time.
60 seconds = 1 minute   60 minutes = 1 hour

A minute is also a unit for measuring angles.
60 minutes = 1 degree of angle measure

missing addend

A missing addend is a number that tells what must be added to one given number to equal another given number.

Example
Grant had saved $60. He wanted a new bicycle that cost $100. How much more money did he need to buy the bicycle?
60 + ☐ = 100
The missing addend is 40. Grant needed $40 to buy the bicycle.

mixed number

A mixed number has both a whole number and a fractional part.

Examples
$1\frac{1}{2}$ $3\frac{3}{5}$ $23\frac{4}{7}$

See also decimal mixed number.

mode

The mode is the number that occurs most often in a set of numbers. Some sets of numbers have more than one mode and some sets have no mode.

Example (one mode for a set of numbers)
Set of numbers: 1, 3, 3, 4, 7, 8
Mode: 3

Example (more than one mode for a set of numbers)
Set of numbers: 1, 3, 3, 4, 7, 7, 8
Modes: 3, 7

Example (no mode for a set of numbers)
Set of numbers: 1, 3, 4, 7, 8
Mode: None

See also average.

motif

A motif is a shape that is repeated in a design.

See also tessellation.

multiple

A multiple is the product of a given number and another whole number.

Examples
Multiples of 4 include 0, 4, 8, 12, . . .
($4 \times 0 = 0$; $4 \times 1 = 4$; $4 \times 2 = 8$; $4 \times 3 = 12$; . . .)
Multiples of 6 include 0, 6, 12, 18, . . .
($6 \times 0 = 0$; $6 \times 1 = 6$; $6 \times 2 = 12$; $6 \times 3 = 18$; . . .)

multiplication

Multiplication is one of the four basic operations on numbers. Multiplication can be explained by using several different situations. Some of these situations are repeated addition, array, area, and combinations.

Example (repeated addition)
There are 3 cookies on each of 4 plates.
$4 \times 3 = 3 + 3 + 3 + 3 = 12$
There are 12 cookies in all.

Example (array)
There are 3 rows and 4 columns.
$3 \times 4 = 12$
There are 12 cans on the shelf.

Example (area)
The length of the rectangle is 4 units.
The width of the rectangle is 3 units.
$4 \times 3 = 12$
The area of the rectangle is 12 square units.

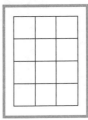

M

multiplication
(continued)

Example (combinations)
Danae was going on a trip. She wanted to pack as many outfits as she could, using as few items of clothing as possible. She packed four shirts: red, green, blue, and yellow. She packed three pairs of pants: denim, tan, and white. How many different outfits can she make?

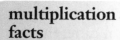

$4 \times 3 = 12$ Danae could make 12 outfits.

See also area; array; basic facts; factor; product.

multiplication facts

The multiplication facts are the 100 multiplication combinations of one-digit numbers.

See also basic facts.

multiplication sentence

A multiplication sentence is a number sentence used to express multiplication.

Examples
$6 \times 4 = 24$
$\frac{1}{2} \times \frac{1}{4} = \frac{1}{8}$

See also number sentence.

multiplication table

A multiplication table is a table that organizes the 100 basic multiplication facts.

See also basic facts.

mutually exclusive events

Mutually exclusive events are events that cannot occur at the same time.

Examples
Being 10 years old and 14 years old at the same time
Being in Chicago and Dallas at the same time
Rolling an odd number and an even number on one die at the same time

natural numbers

Natural numbers are the numbers 1, 2, 3, 4, 5, ... They go on without end. Also called counting numbers.

negative integer

A negative integer is an integer that is less than zero.

See also integers.

negative number

A negative number is any number less than 0. Negative numbers are written with a negative sign (⁻).

Examples
The temperature outside was ⁻4°C.

The lowest point on Earth is found in the Pacific Ocean near Guam. Its elevation is ⁻36,198 feet, or 36,198 feet below sea level.

net

A net is a pattern that can be cut and folded to make a space figure.

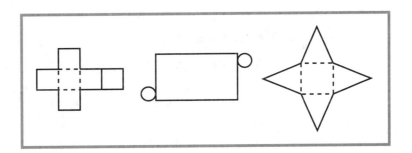

nonterminating decimal

A nonterminating decimal goes on without end.

Examples
$\frac{1}{3}$ may be written as the decimal fraction $0.\overline{3}$. The bar indicates that the 3 continues to repeat itself indefinitely. $0.\overline{3}$ or 0.333. . . is a nonterminating decimal.

$\frac{3}{11}$ may be written in decimal form as $0.\overline{27}$. In this number, the 27 repeats. $0.\overline{27}$ or 0.2727. . . is a nonterminating decimal.

See also terminating decimal.

not equal to (≠)

Read as *is not equal to*. The sign for not equal to (≠) is used to indicate that two numbers do not have the same value.

Example
4 ≠ 5 Read as Four is not equal to five.

See also inequality.

number

A number can be thought of as a concept or an idea used to indicate how many or how much. The number of each set of objects on the right can be named by the numeral 3.

A number can be named in many ways: with words, in standard form, or in expanded form.

Example
word form: two hundred thirty-four
standard form: 234
expanded form: 200 + 30 + 4

Did You Know?

The concept of number is so abstract that a general mathematical definition has not been written for this term. Mathematicians worked for many, many years to find the words to define *number* accurately. Finally, they decided that the best way was to use a specific example. Although many people use the word *number* to mean *numeral*, they are not the same. Numerals are used to represent numbers, and one number can be represented with many different numerals.

See also approximate number; cardinal number; compatible numbers; composite number; counting numbers; decimal mixed number; even number; expanded form; figurate number; fractional number; integers; irrational number; mixed number; numeral; odd number; ordinal number; pentagonal number; perfect number; polygonal numbers; prime number; rational number; rectangular number; square number; standard form; triangular number; whole numbers; word form.

N

number line

A number line is a line or line segment or ray on which numbers are assigned points.

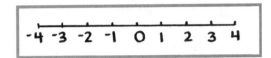

number pattern

A number pattern is a series of numbers arranged or repeated in some order or design. Also called number sequence.

Examples

Pattern of odd numbers: 1, 3, 5, 7, 9, 11, . . .

Pattern of multiples of 3:   0, 3, 6, 9, 12, 15, . . .

Pattern of powers of 2:   2, 4, 8, 16, 32, 64, . . .

Fibonacci sequence: 1, 1, 2, 3, 5, 8, 13, . . .

Did You Know?

The Fibonacci sequence is named for an Italian mathematician named Leonardo Fibonacci, who lived about 800 years ago. This sequence can be found in many living things. For example, if you count the seeds in the spirals of a sunflower, you will find adjacent numbers in the Fibonacci sequence.

See also pattern.

number sense

Number sense is an understanding of numbers. It includes ideas related to number meanings, number relationships and size, and the relative effects of operations on numbers.

Did You Know?

Developing number sense is a lifelong process and is never completely learned. For example, many adults have difficulty giving real-life examples for numbers such as 100, 1000, and so on.

N

number sentence

A number sentence is used to express an arithmetic operation. It is written by using numerals to represent numbers.

Examples
addition sentence: $5 + 3 = 8$
subtraction sentence: $6 - 4 = 2$
multiplication sentence: $7 \times 8 = 56$
division sentence: $8 \div 2 = 4$

See also equation.

numeral

A numeral is a symbol that names a number. There are many different ways numerals can be used to name the same number.

Examples (for 8)
with a digit   **8**
with the addition operation   **5 + 3**
with the division operation   **16 ÷ 2**
with Roman numerals   **VIII**
with tally marks

See also Roman numerals.

numeration system

A numeration system is an organized way of writing the numerals for numbers.

Did You Know?

The Egyptians developed a system based on groups of ten about 5000 years ago. The decimal numeration system we now use, called the Hindu-Arabic numeration system, combines groups of ten, place value, and the use of zero to allow for many complex mathematical ideas and operations.

1 = | (staff)	1,000 = (lotus flower)
10 = (heel)	10,000 = (bent finger)
100 = (coil)	100,000 = (tadpole)
	1,000,000 = (man with raised arms)

IIII (symbols)

4 + 50 + 200 = 254

See also decimal numeration system and Roman numerals.

numerator

The numerator is the name of the upper of the two terms of a common fraction. It is the counting number in a fraction. It tells how many fractional parts in a whole or set have been counted. It also has other meanings. For example, it is the first term in a ratio.

$$\frac{3}{5}$$

Notice that the numerator is written above the fraction bar.

Example
In this picture, 1 is the numerator.

See also common fraction; fraction bar; terms.

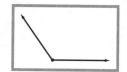

obtuse angle

An obtuse angle is an angle that measures more than 90° but less than 180°.

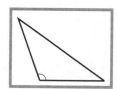

Did You Know?

Obtuse comes from a Latin word meaning "blunted" or "dull" (the opposite of "acute" or "sharp"). The vertex of an obtuse angle is "dull" when compared with the vertex of an acute angle.

See also acute angle; angle; right angle; straight angle.

obtuse triangle

An obtuse triangle is a triangle with an obtuse angle (an angle greater than 90°).

See also acute triangle; right triangle; triangle.

octagon

An octagon is a polygon with eight sides. (*Octa-* is a Greek prefix meaning "eight.")

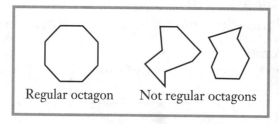

Regular octagon   Not regular octagons

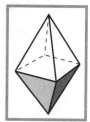

See also polygon.

octahedron

An octahedron is a space figure with eight faces. If each face is an equilateral triangle, then it is one of the five regular polyhedra.

See also polyhedron.

odd number

An odd number is a whole number that cannot be grouped in twos. There is always a remainder of 1 when an odd number is divided by 2.

Odd numbers have 1, 3, 5, 7, or 9 in the ones place.

See also even number.

one-dimensional

A line, ray, or line segment is one-dimensional. The one dimension of a line, ray, or line segment is length.

| Line | Ray | Line segment |

See also geometric figure; three-dimensional; two-dimensional; zero-dimensional.

open sentence

An open sentence is a mathematical sentence for which more information is needed. The information is needed to be able to tell whether the sentence is true or false.

Example
$4 + \square = 9$

statement If a number is used to replace the $\square$ in the example, the open sentence becomes a statement that can be identified as true or false. Writing an open sentence can be helpful in problem solving.

Examples
Michelle spent $15 at the camp store. She bought a T-shirt for $8. How much did she spend for other items?
$8 + \square = 15$ She spent $7 for other items.

After Michelle's trip to the camp store, she had $.75 left in coins. She had only dimes and nickels, and she had the same number of each. How many dimes and how many nickels did she have? Since a dime is equal to $.10, and a nickel is equal to $.05, we can write the following open sentence.

The $\square$ represents the number we do not know.
$(\square \times 10) + (\square \times 5) = 75$
By trying different numbers for both $\square$, we can solve the problem, making the mathematical sentence a true statement.

operation

An operation is an action upon numbers that results in a single number. The arithmetic operations of addition, subtraction, multiplication, and division are operations on two numbers.

operation
(continued)

Examples

$4 + 2 = 6$ $7 \times {}^-3 = {}^-21$

$12 - 3 = 9$ $\frac{1}{4} \div \frac{1}{2} = \frac{1}{2}$

An operation can also be performed on a single number.

Example

$4^2 = 16$

See also addition; basic operations; division; exponent; multiplication; subtraction.

opposite integers

Opposite integers are two integers that are the same distance from 0 on the number line, but in the opposite direction. The set of integers consists of all the whole numbers, their opposites, and zero.

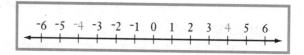

See also integers; opposite of a number.

opposite of a number

The opposite of a number is a number that is the same distance from 0 on the number line as the given number, but in the opposite direction. Also called additive inverse.

Examples

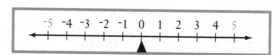

+5 is the opposite of ⁻5, and ⁻5 is the opposite of +5.
(+5 and ⁻5 are called opposites, or opposite integers.)

+3.5 and ⁻3.5 are opposites.
The sum of a number and its opposite is 0.

See also additive inverse.

opposite operations

Opposite operations are two operations, each of which "undoes" the other. Addition and subtraction are opposite operations. Also called inverse operations.

opposite operations (continued)	*Example* 4 + 3 = 7 7 − 3 = 4

Multiplication and division are also opposite operations.

Example
6 × 5 = 30
30 ÷ 5 = 6

See also fact family.

opposite sides and angles in a quadrilateral

In a quadrilateral, opposite sides do not have a common vertex.

Line segments AB and CD are opposite sides in this quadrilateral. Line segments AD and BC are also opposite sides.

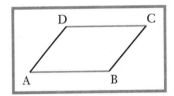

In a quadrilateral, opposite angles do not have a common side.

Angle A and angle C are opposite angles in this quadrilateral. Angle B and angle D are also opposite angles.

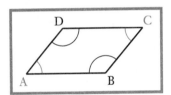

opposite sides and angles in a triangle

In a triangle, a side and an angle are opposite each other if the other two sides are sides of the angle.

Line segment AB is opposite angle C.

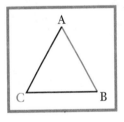

ordered pair

An ordered pair is a set of two numbers that identifies a location on a map or in a coordinate system.

Sometimes a map will use a letter to represent one of the numbers in the ordered pair.

On the next page locate (A, 4).

Now find the White House.

Locate (3, 7).

Now locate (7, 3).

Notice how the order of the numbers in the ordered pair makes a difference in the location of the point.

ordered pair
(continued)

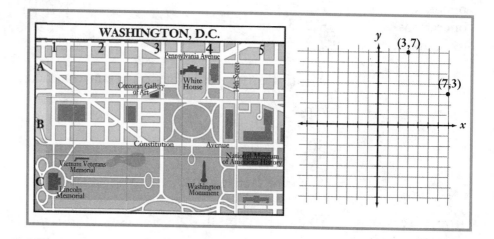

See also coordinate system.

order of operations

Order of operations is an order, agreed upon by mathematicians, for performing operations to simplify expressions. This order is as follows.

First, perform all operations within parentheses or other grouping symbols.

Second, simplify expressions involving exponents.

Third, multiply and divide in order from left to right.

Fourth, add and subtract in order from left to right.

Examples

$10^2 \div (8 \times 2 - 6) + 1$ $3 \div 3 + 3 \times 3 - 3$
$10^2 \div (16 - 6) + 1$ $1 + 9 - 3$
$10^2 \div 10 + 1$ $10 - 3$
$100 \div 10 + 1$ 7
$10 + 1$
11

order property

The order property means that changing the order of the numbers used in an operation does not change the result of that operation. Addition and multiplication have the order property, but subtraction and division do not. Also called commutative property.

See also commutative property of addition; commutative property of multiplication.

order property of addition

The order property of addition means that changing the order in which numbers are added does not change the sum. Also called commutative property of addition.

order property of multiplication

The order property of multiplication means that changing the order in which numbers are multiplied does not change the product. Also called commutative property of multiplication.

ordinal number

An ordinal number is a number used to tell order, or position. (The root word of *ordinal* is *order*.)
Each ordinal number can be paired with a cardinal number.

Examples

Ordinal Number	Cardinal Number
first	one, or 1
second	two, or 2
third	three, or 3
fourth	four, or 4
tenth	ten, or 10
twenty-first	twenty-one, or 21
hundredth	one hundred, or 100

See also cardinal number.

origin

In a coordinate system, the origin is the point of intersection of the *x*- and *y*-axes.

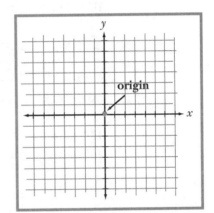

On a number line, the origin is the point assigned to zero.

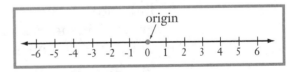

See also coordinate system; number line; *x*- and *y*-axes.

ounce (oz)

An ounce is a unit of weight in the customary system of measurement.
16 ounces = 1 pound

fluid ounce   An ounce (sometimes called fluid ounce) is also a unit of capacity in the customary system of measurement.
8 ounces (or 8 fluid ounces) = 1 cup

Did You Know?

A hen's egg such as one you might eat for breakfast weighs about 2 ounces. A hummingbird's egg, however, is very tiny. It weighs about $\frac{1}{50}$ ounce.

See also customary system of measurement; fluid ounce.

outcome

An outcome is a result of a probability experiment.

possible outcomes There are two possible outcomes of tossing a penny—heads or tails.

equally likely outcomes If a penny is tossed, the equally likely outcomes are heads and tails. That is, either of these two possible outcomes is equally likely. Since there are two equally likely outcomes and heads is one of them, the expected probability of the penny landing heads up is $\frac{1}{2}$. Toss a penny 10 times to see how many times it lands heads up.

favorable outcomes Let's say the penny landed heads up 6 times. Since you were experimenting to see how many times it would land heads up, there were 6 favorable outcomes for your experiment. The experimental probability was $\frac{6}{10}$, or $\frac{3}{5}$.

See also equally likely outcomes; favorable outcome; possible outcomes; probability.

outlier

On a line plot, an outlier is a data category some distance away from other data categories.

line plot A line plot is a graph that shows each item of information on a number line.

In this line plot, 7 is an outlier.

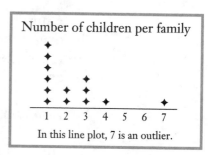
Number of children per family

In this line plot, 7 is an outlier.

oval

An oval is a plane shape that looks like a "flattened" circle.

See also ellipse.

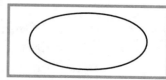

palindrome

A palindrome is a number that reads the same from left to right and from right to left. Also called palindromic number.

Examples
878   342.243   2002

Did You Know?

Words and sentences can be palindromes, too. Both the first and last names of this person are palindromes:
Bob Otto

parallel lines

Parallel lines are lines in the same plane that never intersect. Line segments and rays that are parts of parallel lines are also parallel.

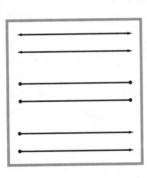

parallelogram

A parallelogram is a quadrilateral with opposite sides parallel.

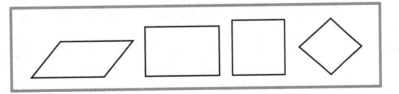

See also quadrilateral.

parallel planes

Parallel planes are planes in space that never intersect.

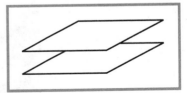

See also plane.

parentheses ( )

Parentheses ( ) are used in mathematics as grouping symbols for operations. When simplifying an expression, the operations within the parentheses are performed first.

Example
$(2 + 3) \times 4$
5×4
20

See also order of operations.

partial product

A partial product is one part of the result when multiplying numbers with more than one digit.

Example
$$124$$
$$\underline{\times 3}$$

$12 \ (3 \times 4)$
$60 \ (3 \times 20)$ $\Big\}$ partial products
$\underline{300} \ (3 \times 100)$
372 (the sum of the partial products)

See also algorithm.

partition division

In partition division, a number is divided into equal parts. Also called sharing and partitive division.

Example
Daynna, Taylor, and John went blueberry picking. Together, they picked 15 pints. When they got ready to go home, they shared the blueberries equally. How many pints did each person have?
$15 \div 3 = 5$
Each person's share of blueberries was 5 pints.

pattern

A pattern is a repeated sequence or design. Patterns occur everywhere in mathematics as well as in other everyday situations. Patterns in numbers and geometry provide examples of patterns in mathematics.

pattern
(continued)

In some number patterns, the difference between any two consecutive numbers is the same. This kind of pattern is called an arithmetic sequence.

Example
0, 2, 4, 6, 8, 10, 12, . . .
This is the pattern of even numbers. Notice that the pattern begins with 0 and the difference in any two consecutive numbers, or terms, is 2.

1, 3, 5, 7, 9, 11, . . .
This is the pattern of odd numbers. Notice that the pattern begins with 1 and the difference in any two consecutive numbers, or terms, is 2.

0, 6, 12, 18, 24, 30, 36, . . .
This is the pattern of whole-number multiples of 6. Notice that the pattern begins with 0 and the difference in any two consecutive terms is 6.

Some number patterns are not arithmetic sequences.

Examples
1, 4, 9, 16, 25, . . .
2, 6, 18, 54, . . .
1, 1, 2, 3, 5, 8, 13, 21, . . .

geometry patterns Some geometry patterns are visual patterns, or patterns you can see.

Example

This picture is an example of a tessellation. A tessellation is a pattern of shapes that are repeated to fill a plane. The shapes do not overlap and there are no gaps. Other patterns in geometry are formed by relationships among attributes.

Example
These figures are parallelograms because they fit the pattern formed by these two attributes:
They have four sides.
Opposite sides are parallel.

See also arithmetic sequence; tessellation.

pentagon

A pentagon is a polygon with five sides.

Example
The Pentagon Building, on the Potomac River just across from Washington, D.C., is one of the world's largest office buildings. It is built in the shape of a pentagon.

See also polygon.

pentagonal number

A pentagonal number is a whole number that can be shown in an array that looks like a pentagon. Arrays for the first five pentagonal numbers are shown.

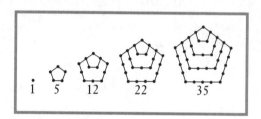

See also polygonal numbers.

percent (%)

Percent (%) is a ratio that represents parts per hundred. It is one way of expressing a fractional number. Common fractions and decimal fractions are two other ways of expressing fractional numbers.

Examples
The sales tax in some states is 5 percent. This is an amount equal to 5 cents in sales tax for every 100 cents (or $.05 per $1.00).

The air we breathe is about 21% oxygen, 78% nitrogen, and 1% argon and other gases.

Nitrogen 78%

Oxygen 21%

Argon and other gases 1%

See also fractional number.

perfect number

A perfect number is a number for which the sum of its proper factors is equal to the number itself.

perfect number
(continued)

proper factor The proper factors of a number are all its factors except the number itself.

Example
6 is a perfect number because the sum of its proper factors (1 , 2, and 3) is equal to 6.

perimeter

Perimeter is the distance around a shape or figure.

Example
Perimeter is also the name for the outer edge of a figure or shape.

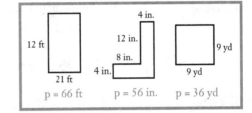

p = 66 ft	p = 56 in. p = 36 yd

circumference Circumference is a special kind of perimeter. It is the distance around a circle.

period

In large numbers, periods are groups of three digits separated by commas. When large numbers are separated into periods, they are easier to read.

Example

Trillions			Billions			Millions			Thousands			Ones		
hundreds	tens	ones	hundreds	tens	ones	hundreds	tens	ones	hundreds	tens	ones	hundreds	tens	ones
						2	6	5	4	2	0	3		

Numbers are sometimes separated into periods by spaces instead of commas.

Example
1 000 000 (read as one million)

perpendicular

Perpendicular means "meeting at right angles." Lines, rays, line segments, and planes can be perpendicular.

Examples
Perpendicular lines, rays, and line segments are lines or parts of lines that meet or cross at right angles.

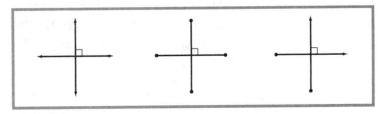

perpendicular lines

Perpendicular lines are lines that meet at right angles. In everyday language, parts of lines (rays and line segments) that meet at right angles are sometimes called perpendicular lines.

See also perpendicular.

perpendicular planes

Perpendicular planes are planes that meet or cross at right angles.

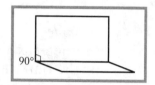

See also perpendicular.

pi (π)

Pi (π) is the ratio of the circumference of a circle to its diameter. The value of pi is 3.1416 . . . , an irrational number. 3.14 and $3\frac{1}{7}$ (or $\frac{22}{7}$) are often used as approximate values for pi. Pi is a constant value. That is, the ratio of the circumference to the diameter is the same for all circles.

This drawing shows the circumference of the circle "stretched out." It is a little more than three diameters in length.

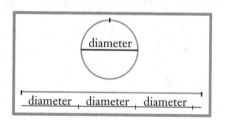

See also circumference.

picture graph

A picture graph is a kind of bar graph that uses pictures or drawings to show information. Also called pictogram and pictograph.

See also bar graph.

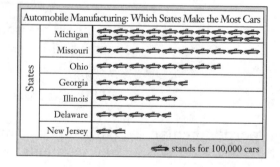

pie graph

A pie graph is a graph in the shape of a pie, or circle, that shows how a total amount has been divided into parts. The pie, or circle, represents the total amount. The slices of pie show how the total amount has been divided. Also called circle graph and pie chart.

See also circle graph.

pint (pt)

Pint is a unit of capacity in the customary system of measurement.

2 cups = 1 pint   2 pints = 1 quart

See also capacity; customary system of measurement.

place value

Place value is the value of a digit determined by its position in a number. In the decimal numeration system, the numeration system we use almost all the time, place value is based on groupings of ten and powers of ten.

Example
In the number 3487, 8 represents 8 tens and is said to be in the tens place.

thousands	hundreds	tens	ones
3	4	8	7

Did You Know?

Computer scientists use a numeration system in which place value is based on groupings of two and powers of two. The first five numbers in this system, called the base-two or binary numeration system, are 0, 1, 10, 11, and 100. Their values in base-ten are 0, 1, 2, 3, and 4.

Base-two has only two digits, 0 and 1. Computer scientists use the digits to tell the computer what to do. 0 switches the electric current off, and 1 turns the current on. Through the use of many 0s and 1s, computer scientists can give the computer very complex instructions.

See also decimal numeration system.

plane

A plane is a flat surface that extends infinitely in all directions.

A plane is two-dimensional. It has length and width but no thickness.

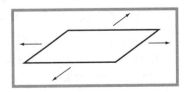

See also plane figure; two-dimensional.

plane figure

A plane figure is a geometric figure that has no thickness. It lies entirely in one plane. Also called plane shape, two-dimensional figure, and two-dimensional shape.

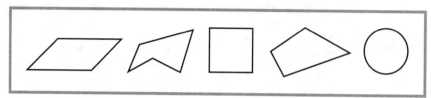

plotting a point

Plotting a point in a coordinate system is locating and marking a point when given its coordinates.

Example
To plot (3, 5), first locate 3 on the *x*-axis and 5 on the *y*-axis. Follow the arrows shown in the drawing.

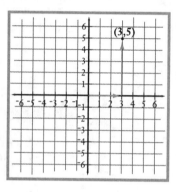

See also coordinate system; ordered pair.

PM

PM is used to label the time between noon and midnight. Also written as P.M., pm, and p.m.

 Did You Know?

P.M. is the abbreviation for *post meridiem*, a Latin phrase meaning "after noon."

point

A point is a location in space.

dimensional A point is zero-dimensional because it does not occupy space. It has neither length, width, nor height. Because a point has no dimensions, we cannot draw a picture of it. We usually represent a point with a dot.

Mathematicians define geometric figures as sets of points.

A
•

See also zero-dimensional.

polygon

A polygon is a closed plane figure formed by line segments.

regular polygon A regular polygon has all sides of equal length and all angles of equal measure.

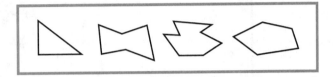

irregular polygon An irregular polygon has sides or angles that are not congruent.

 Did You Know?

Polygon comes from Greek words meaning "many" and "angle."

See also plane figure.

polygonal numbers

Polygonal numbers are numbers that can be represented by arrays that look like various plane figures. Also called figurate numbers.

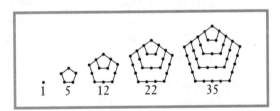

See also pentagonal number; rectangular number; square number; triangular number.

polyhedron

pl. **polyhedra** A polyhedron is a closed space figure with faces that are in the shape of polygons.

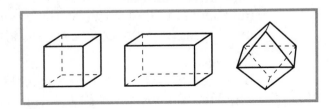

polyhedron
(continued)

regular polyhedra There are five regular polyhedra.

Examples
All the faces of a regular polyhedron are congruent regular polygons, and all the angles are congruent.

Number of faces	4	6	8	12	20
Name	Tetrahedron	Cube	Octahedron	Dodecahedron	Icosahedron
Sketch					
Net					

See also cube; dodecahedron; icosahedron; octahedron; prism; rectangular prism; tetrahedron; triangular prism.

population

In statistics, a population is the total group from which a sample is taken.

Example
A survey found that vanilla was the favorite ice cream flavor for a sample of people in one state. The sample was selected from the population in that state who eat ice cream.

Population also refers to the number of people who live in a specific location.

Examples
The states with the largest and smallest populations are:
Largest: California, with a population of about 30,000,000
Smallest: Wyoming, with a population of about 500,000

positive integer

A positive integer is an integer that is greater than 0.

See also integers.

positive number

A positive number is any number greater than 0. Positive numbers may be written with the positive sign (+). A nonzero number written without a sign is also positive.

Examples
Body temperature for humans is 98.6°F. The elevation of Mt. McKinley is +20,320 feet, or 20,320 feet above sea level.

possible outcomes

Possible outcomes are the possible results of a probability experiment.

Example
When a penny is tossed to see which way it lands, there are two possible outcomes—heads or tails.

See also outcome; sample space.

pound (lb)

A pound is a unit of weight in the customary system of measurement.

Example
1 pound = 16 ounces

The pound is also a unit of money in Great Britain and several other countries.

Did You Know?

The abbreviation lb comes from libra, a Latin word meaning "pound."

See also customary system of measurement; weight.

power of a number

The power of a number is the number of times a number is used as a factor. It is usually indicated by an exponent.

Examples
$10^2 = 10 \times 10 = 100$, or 10 to the second power
$2^3 = 2 \times 2 \times 2 = 8$, or 2 to the third power

See also exponent.

predict

To predict is to make a reasonable statement about what might happen.

Example
Chris tossed a penny nine times. It landed heads up six times. The last three tosses were heads. Chris might have made any of the following predictions about the outcome of the tenth toss.
a. The penny will land heads because it landed heads the last three tosses.
b. The penny will land tails because it landed heads the last three tosses.
c. The penny has an equal chance of landing heads or tails.

He chose c because he knew that, when tossing a penny, heads and tails are equally likely outcomes.

prime factor

A prime factor is a prime number that is a factor of a whole number.

Example
The factors of 12 are 1, 2, 3, 4, and 6.
Of these factors, 2 and 3 are prime factors.

See also factor; prime factorization; prime number.

prime factorization

Prime factorization is the expression of a composite number as the product of its prime factors. Also called complete factorization.

Example
The order of factors varies, but these three factor trees all give the same result. The prime factorization of 24 is $2 \times 2 \times 2 \times 3$ (or $2^3 \times 3$). Every composite number has only one prime factorization and can be expressed with prime factors.

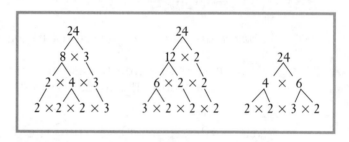

See also factor tree; prime factor; prime number.

prime number

A prime number is a counting number that has exactly two factors, 1 and itself.

Examples
$5 = 1 \times 5$
$19 = 1 \times 19$
The number 1 has only one factor ($1 \times 1 = 1$).
It is not a prime number.
It is also not a composite number.

See also composite number; prime factorization.

principal

Principal is an amount of money borrowed or loaned.

See also interest.

prism

A prism is a space figure with two parallel bases that are polygons of the same size and shape. It has rectangles or other parallelograms for all other faces. A prism is named by the shape of its bases.

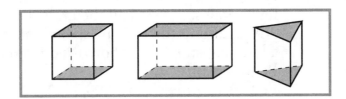

See also rectangular prism; triangular prism.

probability

Probability is the likelihood, or chance, that a given event will occur. Probability is represented with a fractional number between 0 and 1. The closer to 1, the more likely the event is to occur. The closer to 0, the less likely the event is to occur. Also called chance.

Examples
The probability that there will be school on Monday during nine months of the year is close to 1. The probability of snow in Arizona during July is close to 0. The probability that a penny will land on its head, if tossed, is $\frac{1}{2}$.

See also compound event; dependent event; independent events; outcome.

problem

A problem is a situation in which all three of the following are true:
You want or need to find a solution.
You do not already know how to find the solution.
You are willing to try to find the solution.
Learning to solve problems is the major reason for studying mathematics.

product

A product is the result of multiplication.

Example
$5 \times 6 = 30$
factor $\times$ factor = product

See also factor; factor pair; multiplication.

profit

In business transactions, profit is the amount of money left after all expenses are paid.

Example
Pedro made some crafts to sell at the craft fair. He paid $15.43 for supplies. He sold all the crafts he made for $22.00. Not counting the time he spent making the crafts or the additional supplies he borrowed from his mother, what was Pedro's profit?
Pedro's income was $22.00.
Pedro's expenses were $15.43.
$22.00 - 15.43 = 6.57$
Pedro's profit was $6.57.

proper factors

The proper factors of a number are all its factors except the number itself.

Example
The proper factors of 20 are 1, 2, 4, 5, and 10.

See also factor.

proper fraction

A proper fraction is a common fraction that names a number less than 1.

Examples
$\frac{1}{2}, \frac{3}{4}, \frac{3}{15}, \frac{99}{100}$

For each proper fraction, the numerator is less than the denominator.

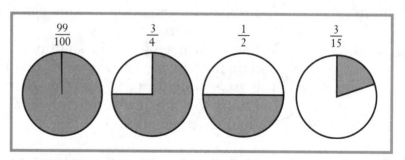

proportion

A proportion is a statement that two ratios are equal. Proportions can be written as equivalent fractions or as equal ratios.

Examples
$\frac{3}{4} = \frac{12}{16}$
$1:2 = 7:14$

proportion (continued)	There are four terms of a proportion. A proportion may be written $\frac{a}{b} = \frac{c}{d}$ or $a:b = c:d$. The terms are a, b, c, and d. The extremes are a and d, and the means are b and c. The product of the means and the product of the extremes are equal.

Example
Proportion: $1:2 = 7:14$. Note that $2 \times 7 = 1 \times 14$.

See also equal ratios; scale.

protractor

A protractor is a tool used to measure angles.

See also angle.

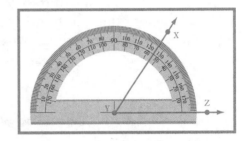

pyramid

A pyramid is a space figure that has any polygon for a base and triangles for all other faces.

apex The triangular faces meet at a point, or vertex, called the apex. A pyramid is named by the shape of its base.

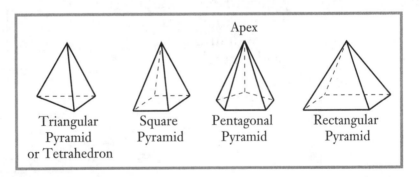

Apex

Triangular Pyramid or Tetrahedron   Square Pyramid   Pentagonal Pyramid   Rectangular Pyramid

 Did You Know?

The pyramids of Egypt served as tombs for ancient Egyptian kings. Pyramids are sometimes used in modern construction, as in the Louvre at right.

P

quadrant

A quadrant is one of the four sections of a rectangular coordinate plane. The quadrants are separated by the *x*- and *y*-axes. The quadrants are numbered in order from I to IV, starting in the upper right quadrant and going counterclockwise.

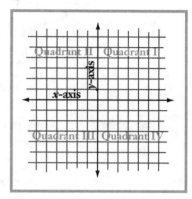

Did You Know?

The first part of the word *quadrant* is like the first part of *quadrilateral* and *quart*. This part of the three words is from a Latin root meaning "four."

See also coordinate system.

quadrilateral

A quadrilateral is a polygon that has four sides. These figures are all quadrilaterals.

See also polygon.

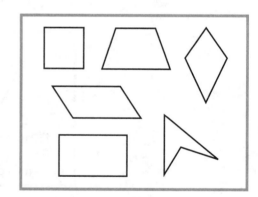

quadrillion

A quadrillion is equal to 1000 trillions. In standard form, one quadrillion is written as 1,000,000,000,000,000. With an exponent, one quadrillion may be written as 1×10^{15} (or simply as 10^{15}).

quart (qt)

A quart is a unit of capacity in the customary system of measurement. A quart is usually used to measure liquids.

In liquid measure: 1 quart = 4 cups or 2 pints
4 quarts = 1 gallon

quart
(continued)

dry quart A dry quart is used to measure dry products such as grains, strawberries, and other fruits. It is a little larger than the quart used in liquid measure.

In dry measure: 1 dry quart = 2 pints
8 dry quarts = 1 peck
4 pecks = 1 bushel

See also customary system of measurement.

quarter-hour

A quarter-hour is a unit of time equal to 15 minutes.

8:15 is a quarter-hour later than 8:00.

Did You Know?

Notice the *quart* in *quarter*. There are four quarts in a gallon, four quarters in a dollar, four quarter-hours in an hour, and four quarters in a football game. *Quart* comes from a Latin word meaning "four" or "fourth."

quotient

A quotient is the number resulting from division.

Examples
In 12 ÷ 3 = 4,
12 is the dividend.
3 is the divisor.
4 is the quotient.

$$\overset{6\ R2}{4\overline{)26}},$$

In 4)26,
26 is the dividend.
4 is the divisor.
6 is the quotient.
2 is the remainder.

See also dividend; division; divisor; remainder.

radius

pl. **radii** The radius of a circle is any line segment from the center of the circle to a point on the circle.

The radius of a sphere is any line segment from the center of the sphere to a point on the sphere.

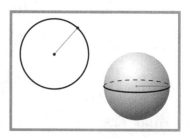

random

Random means "happening by chance."

See also probability.

range   In statistics, the range is the difference between the greatest number and the least number in a set of data.

Example
Ritchie earned these scores in his gymnastics events.

- Floor exercise   9.4
- Pommel horse   9.7
- Rings   9.5
- Vault   9.2

The greatest number is 9.7.
The least number is 9.2.
To find the range, subtract the least number from the greatest.
9.7 − 9.2 = 0.5
The range in Ritchie's scores is 0.5.

See also estimation strategies; rounding; statistics.

rate

A rate is a ratio that compares two quantities expressed in different kinds of units.

Examples
3 pens cost $1.19.
Items (pens) are one kind of unit; money ($1.19) is another.

A jet may travel at the rate of 1000 miles per hour.
Distance (miles) is one kind of unit; time (hour) is another.

The speed of light in space is 186,000 miles per second.
Distance (miles) is one kind of unit; time (second) is another.

The rate of interest on a loan for a new car was advertised at 5.9% per year. This is a complex kind of rate. It compares a rate (percent) with another kind of unit, time (year).

See also interest; unit price.

ratio

A ratio is a comparison of two quantities using a fraction or division.

Example
Three children can sit in each seat on a school bus.
The ratio of children to seats is $\frac{3}{1}$ or 3:1.
Notice that ratios can be written in two ways: $\frac{a}{b}$ or *a:b*
(*b* does not equal 0).
The first term of the ratio is *a* and the second term is *b*.

See also common fraction; equal ratios.

rational number

A rational number is a number that can be written in the form of a common fraction.

Examples
$$\frac{1}{4}, \frac{2}{3}, \frac{4}{2}, \frac{6}{1}, \frac{-10}{2}$$
A rational number can also be written in the form of a decimal fraction that either terminates or repeats.

Examples
0.25
$0.6\overline{6}$

ray

A ray is a part of a line that has one end point and extends infinitely in one direction.

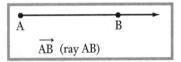

Example
This number line showing whole numbers is really not a line in geometry, but a ray. It begins at the end point, 0, and extends infinitely. (There is no greatest whole number.)

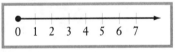

 Did You Know?

A ray of sunshine begins at the sun (the end point) and travels through space in one direction. A ray from the sun can be used as a model for thinking about a ray in geometry.

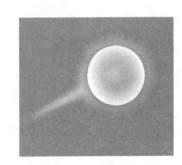

See also line.

real graph

A real graph is a kind of bar graph that uses the real objects being graphed.

See also bar graph.

reciprocal

The reciprocal of a rational number is the number that when used as a factor with the given number will result in a product of 1. Also called multiplicative inverse.

Examples

Rational Number	Reciprocal	Equation
$\frac{1}{4}$	$\frac{4}{1}$	$\frac{1}{4} \times \frac{4}{1} = 1$
$\frac{7}{8}$	$\frac{8}{7}$	$\frac{7}{8} \times \frac{8}{7} = 1$
$\frac{3}{1}$	$\frac{1}{3}$	$\frac{3}{1} \times \frac{1}{3} = 1$
2	$\frac{1}{2}$	$2 \times \frac{1}{2} = 1$

In the following equation, $\frac{b}{a}$ is the reciprocal.

$$\frac{a}{b} \times \frac{b}{a} = 1$$

rectangle

A rectangle is a closed plane figure with four sides and four right angles.

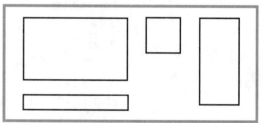

 Did You Know?

A rectangle in which the ratio of length to width is approximately 8 to 5 is called a Golden rectangle. It is considered very pleasing to the eye.

The face of the Parthenon is a Golden rectangle.

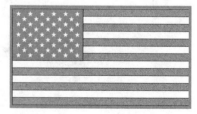

The United States flag is also in the shape of a Golden rectangle.

Related word rectangular

See also parallelogram.

rectangular coordinate system

The rectangular coordinate system is a system used to locate points in a plane. Also called Cartesian coordinate system.

See also coordinate system.

rectangular number

A rectangular number is a whole number that can be shown in an array that looks like a rectangle.

Examples
Arrays for two rectangular numbers are shown below.

Notice that some rectangular numbers can be shown in more than one way.

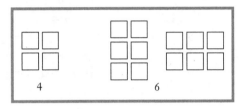

See also pentagonal number; polygonal number; square number; triangular number.

rectangular prism

A rectangular prism is a prism that has rectangles as bases. Also called cuboid and rectangular solid.

See also cube; prism.

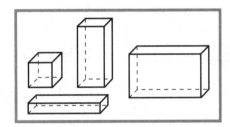

rectangular pyramid

A rectangular pyramid is a pyramid with a rectangle-shaped base.

See also pyramid.

reflection

A reflection is a mirror image of a figure. Also called flip.

See also flip.

reflectional symmetry

A plane figure has reflectional symmetry if it can be divided into two congruent parts that are mirror images. Also called line symmetry.

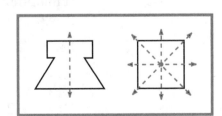

See also symmetry.

regrouping

Regrouping involves changing a number from one form to an equivalent form. This procedure is helpful in doing arithmetic computations. Also called trading.

Example
$$\begin{array}{r} 43 \\ -26 \\ \hline \end{array}$$

In long form the regrouping is as follows.
$$\begin{array}{r} 43 = 30 + 13 \\ -26 = 20 + 6 \\ \hline 10 + 7 = 17 \end{array}$$ (One of the tens in 43 is regrouped with the ones.)

In short form, the regrouping is as follows.
$$\begin{array}{r} \overset{1}{\cancel{4}}3 \\ -26 \\ \hline 17 \end{array}$$

regular polygon

A regular polygon is a plane figure with all sides of equal length and all angles of equal measure.

See also polygon.

related facts

Related facts are related addition and subtraction facts or related multiplication and division facts. Also called fact family and related sentences.

Examples

Related addition and subtraction facts using 2, 3, and 5	Related multiplication and division facts using 2, 4, and 8
2 + 3 = 5 3 + 2 = 5	2 × 4 = 8 4 × 2 = 8
5 − 3 = 2 5 − 2 = 3	8 ÷ 4 = 2 8 ÷ 2 = 4

See also basic facts; fact family.

remainder in division

In division, the remainder is the number left when one number does not divide into another number exactly.

remainder as a whole number Often the remainder in division is expressed as a whole number.

Example
Floyd had 10 gumballs. He divided them among 4 people. How many gumballs did each person receive?

10 ÷ 4 = 2 with a remainder of 2
Each person received 2 gumballs, and there were 2 gumballs remaining. (Cutting gumballs into parts does not work very well!)

remainder in division
(continued)

remainder as a common fraction or decimal fraction   In many division problems, the remainder is expressed as a common fraction or a decimal fraction.

Example
Jamie and Roger went on a 10-mile hike. If the trip lasted 4 hours, about how many miles did they hike per hour?

$10 \div 4 = 2\frac{1}{2}$ or 2.5

Jamie and Roger hiked about $2\frac{1}{2}$ miles (or 2.5 miles) per hour. In this situation, the remainder is expressed as $\frac{1}{2}$ or 0.5.

remainder ignored   In some problems, the remainder is ignored.

Example
Bobbi was making bookshelves for her room. She had 8 feet of lumber for shelves. Each bookshelf was 3 feet long. How many shelves could she make?

$8 \div 3 = 2$, with 2 feet of shelving remaining
She could make 2 shelves. The 2 feet of lumber remaining are not enough for another bookshelf.

remainder as the next highest whole number   Sometimes a remainder requires the problem solution to be the next highest whole number.

Example
Ken bought hot-dog buns for the picnic. He needed 60 buns in all. The buns were packaged in bags containing 8 each. How many packages of buns did he need to buy?

$60 \div 8 = 7$ with a remainder of 4
If Ken buys 7 packages of hot-dog buns, he will have only 56 buns, and he needs 60. He will need to buy 8 packages of buns.

See also division; subtraction.

remainder in subtraction

In subtraction, the remainder is the number left in a "take away" situation.

Example
Karl had 15 baseball cards. He gave 9 to Jim. How many baseball cards did he have left?

$15 - 9 = 6$
The remainder is 6, the number of baseball cards Karl had left. (9 cards were "taken away.")

R

repeated addition

Repeated addition is an explanation for multiplication in which the same number is added over and over.

Example
$3 \times 8 = 8 + 8 + 8 = 24$

See also multiplication.

rhombus

pl. **rhombuses** or **rhombi** A rhombus is a parallelogram with all sides congruent.

Examples
In everyday language, some rhombuses are sometimes called diamonds.

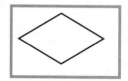

Related word rhomboid

See also parallelogram; square.

right angle (⌐)

A right angle is an angle that measures 90°.

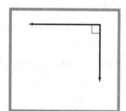

See also acute angle; angle; obtuse angle; straight angle.

right triangle

A right triangle is a triangle with one right angle (90°).

See also triangle.

Roman numeration system

The Roman numeration system is a numeration system that probably developed between 500 B.C. and A.D. 100, during the early years of the Roman Empire. It uses Roman numerals, or letters and combinations of letters, to represent numbers. The following are Roman numerals and their values in the base-ten system.

Roman	I	V	X	L	C	D	M
Base-ten	1	5	10	50	100	500	1000

See also decimal numeration system.

rotation	A rotation is the movement of a figure around a fixed point. Also called turn. *See also* turn.	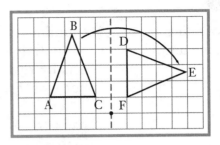

rotational symmetry	A plane figure has rotational symmetry if the shape of the figure moves onto itself when rotated. *See also* symmetry.

rounding

Rounding is a procedure sometimes used in estimating the result of an arithmetic operation.

rounding a whole number Rounding a whole number usually results in a number that is close to the original number and has the same number of digits, but more of the digits are zeros.

Example
During her stay at camp, Anna had 12 hours of horseback riding lessons. She also rode on trail rides for 17 hours. About how many hours did Anna get to ride horses while she was at camp?

12, rounded to the nearest 10, is 10.
17, rounded to the nearest 10, is 20.
10 + 20 = 30
Anna rode a horse about 30 hours while she was at camp.

rounding a common fraction or mixed number One way of rounding a common fraction or common mixed number is to round to the nearest whole number.

Example
While fishing, Barbara caught, measured, and then released two sunfish. The larger one was $5\frac{3}{4}$ inches long, and the smaller one was $4\frac{1}{8}$ inches long.

About how much longer was the larger fish?

$5\frac{3}{4}$, rounded to the nearest whole number, is 6.

$4\frac{1}{8}$, rounded to the nearest whole number, is 4.

6 − 4 = 2

The larger fish was about 2 inches longer than the smaller one.

R

rounding
(continued)

rounding a decimal fraction or decimal mixed number
Rounding a decimal fraction or a decimal mixed number usually results in a number close to the number being rounded, but with fewer digits.

Example
Cliff and his friends bought a large pizza for $11.25. They also bought a small pizza for $5.95. About how much did they pay for both pizzas?
$11.25, rounded to the nearest whole number (or dollar) is $11.
$5.95, rounded to the nearest whole number (or dollar) is $6.
11 + 6 = 17
Cliff and his friends paid about $17 for both pizzas.

See also estimation strategies.

row

A row is an arrangement of items or numbers from left to right in an array or table.

Year	Number of Missions with Astronauts	New Astronauts in Space (first space flight)	Time in Space
1961	♟ ♟	⛷ ⛷	30 minutes
1962	♟ ♟ ♟	⛷ ⛷ ⛷	19 hours
1963	♟	⛷	34 hours
1964			0
1965	♟ ♟ ♟ ♟ ♟	⛷ ⛷ ⛷ ⛷ ⛷	330 hours
1966	♟ ♟ ♟ ♟ ♟	⛷ ⛷ ⛷ ⛷ ⛷	309 hours
1967			0
1968	♟ ♟	⛷ ⛷ ⛷	407 hours
1969	♟ ♟ ♟ ♟	⛷ ⛷ ⛷ ⛷	873 hours
1970	♟	⛷ ⛷	141 hours	←Row
1971	♟ ♟	⛷ ⛷ ⛷ ⛷	511 hours
1972	♟ ♟	⛷ ⛷ ⛷ ⛷	568 hours
1973	♟ ♟ ♟	⛷ ⛷ ⛷ ⛷ ⛷ ⛷	171 days

See also column.

sales tax rate

Sales tax rate is tax expressed as a percent of the price the customer pays for an item. It is added to the price. In most states the sales tax rate is set at the state level. This rate varies from state to state.

Example
Joseph bought a milkshake that cost $1.00. The sales tax rate in his state is 6%. In all, how much did Joseph pay?
6% of 1.00 is .06.
1.00 + .06 = 1.06
Joseph paid $1.06 in all.

sample

A sample consists of all the people or items chosen to represent a larger group. Also called sample group.

See also sampling; population.

sample space

Sample space consists of all the possible outcomes of a probability experiment.

Example
When a coin is tossed, there are two possible outcomes—heads or tails. The sample space for the experiment of tossing a coin is {heads, tails}.

See also outcome.

sampling

Sampling is a process used to select people or items to represent a larger group. Sampling must be carefully done for the sample to be representative of the larger group, or population.

Example
Imagine you want to know the favorite movie of moviegoers in your community. If you survey only the students in your school, your sample is not likely to represent your community. Instead, you need to survey moviegoers of different age levels, different educational backgrounds, different incomes, and so on.

See also sample.

scale (in measurement)

A scale is a series of marks at regular intervals along a line, used for measuring. A scale usually uses a number line.

Examples

Notice that the scales on the thermometer and centimeter ruler are number lines.

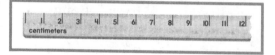

Scale is also the name of a tool for measuring weight.

scale (in graphs)

In a picture graph, the graph scale is the ratio between the picture or icon and the number it represents. In a bar graph or line graph, the graph scale is the ratio between each space on the graph and the number it represents.

Examples
The scale for this picture graph is 1 spaceship = 6 students.

For how long would you like to travel in space?	
0 months	🚀🚀🚀
3 months	🚀🚀🚀🚀🚀🚀🚀🚀🚀🚀
6 months	🚀🚀🚀🚀🚀
12 months	🚀🚀🚀🚀🚀🚀

Each 🚀 stands for 6 students.

The scale for this bar graph is 1 block = $\frac{1}{2}$ hour.

S

scale (in scale drawing)

A scale drawing represents an actual object but is different in size. Scale drawings are usually smaller than the object represented. The scale for a drawing is the ratio between the size of the drawing and what is represented. A map is an example of a scale drawing.

map scale   A map scale is a ratio between the dimensions on the map and the dimensions of the area it represents.

Example
The scale for
this map is
1 inch = 100 miles.

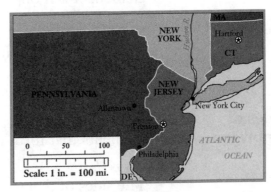

scale model

A scale model is a model of an actual object that is different only in size. Usually it is smaller than the actual object. The scale for a model of an object is the ratio between the size of the model and the size of the actual object.

Example
The scale for this model
train is 1 in. = 3 ft.

See also proportion; ratio; similar figures.

scalene triangle

A scalene triangle is a triangle with all three sides of different lengths.

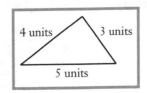

See also triangle.

second

A second is a unit for measuring time. 60 seconds = 1 minute *Second* is also the ordinal number after *first*.

Did You Know?

Television commercial breaks usually last about 30 seconds (or 15 seconds).

set

A set is a collection or group. Sets may contain numbers, objects, or other items.

Examples
Set of people in my family: Matt, Eula, Jamie, Roger
Set of counting numbers: 1, 2, 3, 4, . . .

element Each object of the set is called a member or element.

sharing

Sharing is a form of division in which a number is divided into equal parts. Also called partition division and partitive division.

See also division; partition division.

sides of a polygon

The sides of a polygon are the line segments that form the polygon.

Example
The sides of this triangle are line segments AB, BC, and CA.
(Each line segment is one side.)

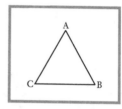

sides of an angle

The sides of an angle are the rays that form the angle.

Example
The sides of this angle are rays AB and CB. (Each ray is one side of the angle.)

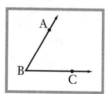

sides of an equation

The sides of an equation are the expressions on either side of the = sign.

Example
$4 + n = 7 - 1$
$4 + n$ is the left side of the equation.
$7 - 1$ is the right side.

similar figures

Similar figures have the same shape but not necessarily the same size. For similar figures, corresponding angles have the same measure, and corresponding sides are proportional.

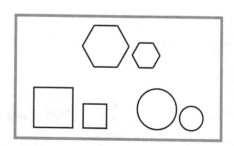

See also congruent figures; proportion; scale.

similar fractions	Similar fractions are fractions with the same denominator. Also called like fractions.

simple closed curve	A simple closed curve is a closed curve that does not cross itself.

See also closed curve.

simplest form	For common fractions, also called lowest terms and lowest terms of a fraction.

of common fractions A common fraction is in simplest form when the greatest common factor of the numerator and the denominator is 1.

Example
To express $\frac{6}{8}$ in simplest form. Think: What is the greatest common factor of 6 and 8? (2) Use 2 as the numerator and denominator of a common fraction ($\frac{2}{2}$). This common fraction is equivalent to 1.

Divide $\frac{6}{8}$ by this value for 1.

$\frac{6}{8} \div \frac{2}{2} = \frac{3}{4}$

Think: What is the greatest common factor of 3 and 4? (1) $\frac{6}{8}$ expressed in simplest form is $\frac{3}{4}$.

of expressions An expression is in simplest form when no terms can be combined.

Example
To express 3 + (2 × 5) in simplest form:
First, perform the operation within parentheses.
2 × 5 = 10
Next, perform the addition.
3 + 10 = 13
3 + (2 × 5) expressed in simplest form is 13.

See also greatest common factor; order of operations.

simplify	To simplify is to express in simplest form.

See also simplest form.

S

skew lines

Skew lines are lines in space that are not in the same plane. They do not intersect and are not parallel.

Imagine the major highway as one line and the road passing over it as another line. These two lines are skew lines.

skip counting

Skip counting is counting by a given whole number greater than 1.

Examples
Skip counting by twos beginning with 2: 2, 4, 6, 8, . . .
Skip counting by fives beginning with 5: 5, 10, 15, . . .
Skip counting by tens beginning with 25: 25, 35, 45, . . .

slide

A slide is the movement of a figure along a line. Also called translation.

See also flip; turn.

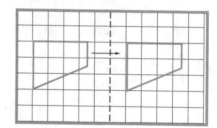

solid

A solid is a shape that has three dimensions. Also called solid figure, space figure, three-dimensional figure, and three-dimensional shape.

See also space figure.

space figure

A space figure is a geometric figure with points in more than one plane. Space figures are three-dimensional. Also called solid, solid shape, three-dimensional figure, and three-dimensional shape.

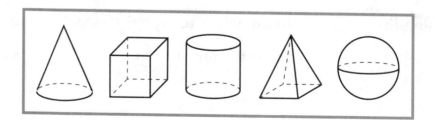

sphere

A sphere is a space figure shaped like a round ball. All points on the sphere are an equal distance from its center.

Did You Know?

The earth is shaped like a sphere that has been flattened at both polar regions. This shape is called an oblate spheroid.

Related words spherical, spheroid

See also hemisphere.

square

A square is a rectangle with all four sides of equal length.

The square of a number (n^2) is the result of multiplying that number by itself.

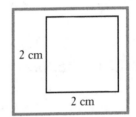

Example
The square of 6 is 6×6, or 36.
Another way of writing the square of 6 is 6^2.
6^2 may be read as *six squared*.
This is a model of 6^2.

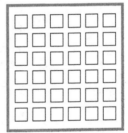

See also exponent; power of a number; rectangle.

square centimeter (cm²)

A square centimeter is equal to the area of a square that measures 1 centimeter on each side.

See also cm²; square unit.

square foot (ft²)

A square foot is equal to the area of a square that measures 1 foot on each side. Also written as sq ft.

See also ft²; square unit.

square inch (in.²)

A square inch is equal to the area of a square that measures 1 inch on each side. Also written as sq in.

See also in.²; square unit.

S

square kilometer (km²)

A square kilometer is equal to the area of a square that measures 1 kilometer on each side.

See also km²; square unit.

square meter (m²)

A square meter is equal to the area of a square that measures 1 meter on each side.

See also m²; square unit.

square mile (mi²)

Also written as sq mi. A square mile is equal to the area of a square that measures 1 mile on each side.

See also mi²; square unit.

square number

A square number is usually thought of as a counting number that can be shown in an array in the shape of a square. It is the result of multiplying some counting number by itself—for example, $5 \times 5 = 25$ (or $5^2 = 25$). In counting numbers, also called perfect square.

Examples
Arrays for the first five square numbers are shown.

See also square.

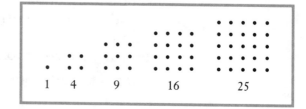

square pyramid

A square pyramid is a pyramid with a square-shaped base.

See also pyramid.

square root (√)

A square root of a number is one of two equal factors of that number.

Examples

A square root of 4 is 2 because $2 \times 2 = 4$.

A square root of 6.25 is 2.5 because $2.5 \times 2.5 = 6.25$

See also square number.

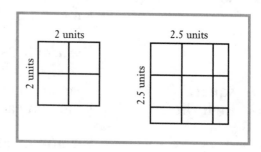

square unit

A square unit is equal to the area of a square with each side measuring 1 unit.

In the customary system of measurement, commonly used square units include in.^{2} (square inch), ft^2 (square foot), yd^2 (square yard), and mi^2 (square mile). In the metric system of measurement, commonly used square units include cm^2 (square centimeter), m^2 (square meter), and km^2 (square kilometer).

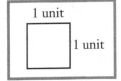

Although a square unit of area is usually thought of in the shape of a square, it can also take other shapes.

Each of these shapes has an area of 1 cm^2.

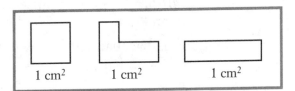

See also area; cm^2; ft^2; in.^{2}; km^2; m^2; mi^2; yd^2.

square yard (yd^2)

Also written as sq yd. A square yard is equal to the area of a square that measures 1 yard on each side.

See also yd^2; square unit.

standard form

Standard form is the usual way of writing the name of a number, with digits. When the standard form of a whole number has more than 4 digits, it is usually written with commas separating groups of three digits, or periods. Also called standard numeral.

Examples
34   807   2720 (may also be written as 2,720)

17,302   2,103,891,762

See also period.

standard system

The standard system of measurement is the system of measurement commonly used in everyday life in the United States. Also called customary measurement system, customary system, customary system of measurement, English measurement system, English system of measurement, and U.S. Customary System.

See also customary system of measurement.

S

statement

A statement is a sentence that can be identified as true or false.

Examples
$4 + 5 = 9$ (true)
$4 + 5 = 3 \times 3$ (true)
Whole numbers include counting numbers.   (true)
A stop sign is in the shape of a hexagon.   (false)
$4 + 5 = 7 + 1$ (false)

statistics

Statistics is the science of collecting, organizing, representing, and interpreting data. The word *statistics* is also often used to mean "data."

This baseball card shows statistics for Babe Ruth.

Related words statistical, statistician

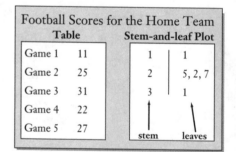

BABE RUTH
PITCHER & OUTFIELDER
Given Name: George Herman Ruth
BORN: Baltimore, MD Feb. 6, 1895
DIED: New York, NY Aug. 16, 1948
HEIGHT: 6'2"   **WEIGHT:** 215 lbs.
BATS: Left   **THROWS:** Left
Baltimore Orioles, Boston Red Socks, New York Yankees, Boston Braves
Started his career in 1914 with the Baltimore Orioles. Joined the Boston Red Sox later that year. Hit 714 homers and had a lifetime average of .342. Ended his career in 1935 with the Boston Braves. One of the first five players elected to the National Baseball Hall of Fame.

Did You Know?

A statistician uses mathematical ideas from the field of statistics to answer questions and solve problems.

stem-and-leaf plot

A stem-and-leaf plot is a type of graph that organizes data so that frequencies can be compared.

The stem-and-leaf plot groups the football scores shown in the table.

1/1 means 11.

2/5, 2, 7 means 25, 22, and 27.

3/1 means 31.

Football Scores for the Home Team

Table		Stem-and-leaf Plot	
Game 1	11	1	1
Game 2	25	2	5, 2, 7
Game 3	31	3	1
Game 4	22		
Game 5	27	stem	leaves

The stem-and-leaf plot shows that scores for most of the games were in the 20s.

straight angle

A straight angle has a measure of 180°. It is also equal to the measure of two right angles.

Its measure is equal to a straight line.

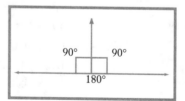

90°   90°
180°

See also angle.

straightedge

A straightedge is a tool used for drawing line segments. Many geometric figures can be constructed with only a straightedge and a compass.

An unmarked ruler is often used as a straightedge.

See also construction.

subtraction

Subtraction is a way of finding answers to the following questions without counting.
• How many are left?
• How many more (or less) are there?
• How many more are needed?

Subtraction is one of the four basic arithmetic operations. (The other basic operations are addition, multiplication, and division.)

remainder In some subtraction problems we find the remainder, or how many are left after some are taken away.

Example
Josh had 5 packs of baseball cards.
He gave 2 packs to Renee.
How many packs did Josh have left?
$5 - 2 = 3$
Josh had 3 packs of baseball cards left (a remainder).

difference In some subtraction problems we need to compare two numbers to find how much more one number is than another. The answer is called a difference.

Example
Will went fishing for 5 hours. David went with him but stayed for only 2 hours. How many more hours did Will fish?
$5 - 2 = 3$
William fished for 3 more hours (the difference).

missing addend Subtraction can help us find a missing addend, or how many more must be added to have the number needed.

Example
Mary has 2 tickets.
She must have 5 tickets to ride the water slide.
How many more tickets does she need?
$2 + \square = 5$
The missing addend is 3, the number of tickets Mary needs.

Related word subtract

See also difference; missing addend; operation; remainder.

S

subtraction sentence

A subtraction sentence is a number sentence used to express subtraction.

Examples
$5 - 3 = 2$
$4\frac{1}{2} - \frac{3}{4} = 3\frac{3}{4}$

See also number sentence.

sum

A sum is the result of addition.

Example
In $3 + 4 = 7$,
3 and 4 are addends.
+ is the symbol for addition.
7 is the sum.

See also addend; addition.

surface area

Surface area is the total area of the surface of a space figure.

The surface area of this rectangular prism is found by adding the areas of all the faces.

survey

A survey is usually a list of questions asked of a sample of people to determine the characteristics of a group. These questions can be asked by methods such as written surveys or telephone surveys. This is an example of a written survey.

1. What is the last movie you saw?

   _____

2. How many movies do you watch each month?_____

3. What is your all-time favorite movie?

   _____

symmetry

In geometry, symmetry describes the balance a figure has. Both plane and space figures may have symmetry.

line symmetry A plane figure has line symmetry if it can be divided into two congruent parts that are mirror images.

rotational symmetry A plane figure has rotational symmetry if, when rotated less than a full turn around a fixed point, the shape of the figure moves onto itself.

Examples

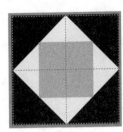 

A space figure has rotational symmetry if the shape of the figure moves onto itself when rotated less than a full turn around a fixed point.

Symmetry is also used to describe the symmetric property of equality.

Examples
If 3 + 4 = 7, then 7 = 3 + 4.
If A = $l \times w$, then $l \times w$ = A.

plane symmetry A space figure has plane symmetry if it can be divided into two halves that are reflections of each other.

Example
A geode can be a model of plane symmetry.

Related words symmetrical, asymmetrical

See also equality; line of symmetry.

S

table

A table is an arrangement of information in rows and columns.

	Land (million sq miles)	Population (millions)	Income per Person (in U.S. dollars)
China	3.7	1,087	330
Mexico	0.76	83.5	1,950
India	1.23	817	260
U.K.	0.09	57.1	8,380

See also column; row.

tablespoon (T)

A tablespoon is a measure of capacity in the customary system of measurement.
1 tablespoon = 3 teaspoons
16 tablespoons = 1 cup

Did You Know?

One or two tablespoons of peanut butter and one tablespoon of jelly spread on bread make a favorite sandwich for many people.

See also customary system of measurement.

tally chart

A tally chart is a chart used to summarize the number of times items occur in a set of data. Also called frequency table.

tally marks

Tally marks are used to record the frequency of an item. Tally marks are also made to count or keep score.

See also frequency table.

tangram

The tangram is a Chinese mathematical puzzle made from a square cut into 7 pieces called tans. These pieces can be used to form many different geometric shapes.

Tangram is also the name of any shape made from all the tans.

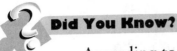
According to legend, a man in ancient China named Tan dropped a porcelain tile, which broke into 7 pieces. Tan spent the rest of his life trying to put the pieces back together again. As he worked with the pieces, he created more than 300 different shapes and pictures, or tangrams.

teaspoon (t)

A teaspoon is a unit of capacity in the customary system of measurement.
3 teaspoons = 1 tablespoon

See also customary system of measurement.

temperature

Temperature is a measure of heat or cold. Temperature is measured in degrees Celsius (°C) in the metric system of measurement. Temperature is measured in degrees Fahrenheit (°F) in the customary system of measurement. The freezing and boiling points of water are used as reference points in both systems.

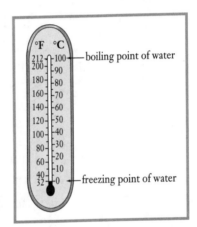

See also Celsius (°C) temperature scale; Fahrenheit (°F) temperature scale.

tenth

A tenth is one of 10 equal parts of a whole or group. One tenth may be written as $\frac{1}{10}$ or 0.1.

Examples

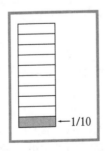

In ordinal numbers, tenth is next after ninth.

See also decimal numeration system.

tenths

Tenths is the name of the place to the right of the decimal point in the decimal numeration system.

In this number, 9 is in the tenths place

ones	.	tenths	hundredths
2	.	9	8

See also decimal numeration system.

terminating decimal

A terminating decimal is a decimal that ends.

Examples
0.5   0.278

terms

The terms of a common fraction are its numerator and denominator.

$$\frac{3}{4} \quad \text{numerator} \atop \text{denominator}$$

There are usually two terms of a ratio. They are called the first term and the second term.

Ratio: $\frac{3}{4}$ or 3:4

3 is the first term and 4 is the second term.

There are four terms of a proportion.
A proportion may be written $\frac{a}{b} = \frac{c}{d}$ or $a{:}b = c{:}d$.
The terms are a, b, c, and d.

Proportion: $\frac{3}{4} = \frac{6}{8}$

The terms of a sequence are the numbers in that pattern or sequence.

Example
2, 4, 8, 16, 32, 64, 128, 256, 512, 1024, . . .

The terms of an expression are the parts of an expression between operation signs.

Expression: $3x + 2$
term   term

See also denominator; numerator; pattern; proportion; ratio; simplest form.

tessellation

A tessellation is a pattern of shapes repeated to fill a plane. The shapes do not overlap and there are no gaps. Also called tiling.

tessellation
(continued)

motif The shape that is repeated, or tessellated, is called a motif.

Related word tessellate
See also pattern.

tetrahedron

A tetrahedron is a space figure with four triangular faces. Also called triangular pyramid.

It is one of the five regular polyhedra.

See also polyhedron.

thousand

A thousand is equal to 1000 ones, 100 tens, or 10 hundreds.

In standard form, one thousand is written as 1000 (or 1,000). With an exponent, one thousand may be written as 1×10^3 (or simply as 10^3).

See also decimal numeration system.

thousandth

A thousandth is one of 1000 equal parts of a whole or a group. One thousandth may be written as $\frac{1}{1000}$ or 0.001.

In ordinal numbers, *thousandth* is next after *nine hundred ninety-ninth*.

thousandths

Thousandths is the name of the next place to the right of hundredths in the decimal numeration system.

In this number, 7 is in thousandths place.

		Ty Cobb's career batting average		
ones	.	tenths	hundredths	thousandths
0	.	3	6	7

See also thousandth; decimal numeration system.

three-dimensional

Three-dimensional is a term used to describe space figures. They occupy space and have volume.

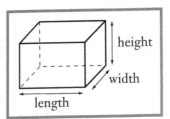

See also geometric figure; one-dimensional; two-dimensional; zero-dimensional.

three-dimensional figure

A three-dimensional figure is a geometric figure that occupies space and has volume. Also called solid, solid figure, solid shape, space figure, and three-dimensional shape.

See also space figure.

tiling

A tiling is a pattern of shapes repeated to fill a plane. The shapes do not overlap and there are no gaps. Also called tessellation.

See also tessellation.

time line

A time line is a number line that is used to show events of history in order.

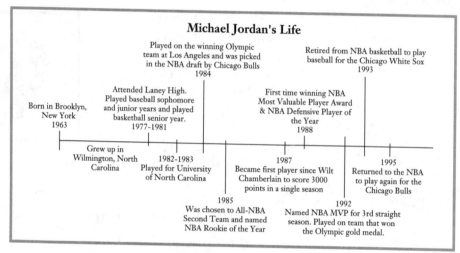

time zone

A time zone is a geographical region throughout which the same standard time is used.

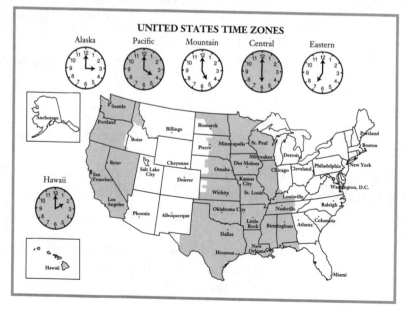

ton (T)

A ton is a unit of weight in both the metric and customary systems of measurement. In the customary system, a ton (T) is equal to 2000 pounds.

metric ton The metric ton (t) is equal to 1000 kilograms.

See also metric ton.

total

The total is all of a quantity or amount.

Examples
In all, 27 students were going on a field trip. Five students could ride in each car. What was the total number of cars needed?
$27 \div 5 = 5$ R2
The total number of cars needed was 6.

Total can also mean "sum" or "to find the sum."
The total (sum) of $2 + 3$ is 5.
Total (find the sum of) the following numbers.
$5 + 3 + 2 + 8$

Related word totality

trading

Trading involves changing a number from one form to an equivalent form.

See also regrouping.

transformation

A transformation is a change in the size, shape, or position of a figure. Transformations that are changes in the position of a figure are called flips (reflections), slides (translations), and turns (rotations).

See also flip; slide; turn.

translation

A translation is the movement of a figure along a line for a given distance. Also called slide.

See also slide.

trapezoid

A trapezoid is a quadrilateral with exactly one set of parallel sides.

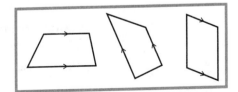

trapezoid
(continued)

isosceles trapezoid If the nonparallel sides are the same length, the trapezoid has a special name: isosceles trapezoid. The trapezoid on the right is an isosceles trapezoid.

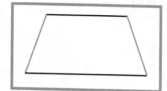

A trapeze is in the shape of a trapezoid.

Related words trapeze; trapezium; trapezoidal
See also quadrilateral.

tree diagram

A tree diagram is a way of organizing possible outcomes so that they are easy to count.

Example
Melissa has two kinds of ice-cream cones (sugar and waffle) and two kinds of ice cream (chocolate and vanilla). How many possible combinations are there if she serves one scoop of ice cream on each cone?

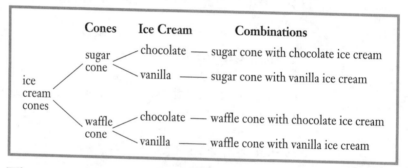

There are four possible combinations.

triangle

A triangle is a plane shape that has three sides and three angles. Triangles are usually named either by their sides or their angles. These triangles are named by their sides.

equilateral triangle All three sides of an equilateral triangle are equal in length.

isosceles triangle Two of the sides of an isosceles triangle are equal in length.

scalene triangle No side of a scalene triangle is equal in length to any other side.

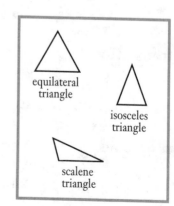

triangle
(continued)

These triangles are named by their angles.

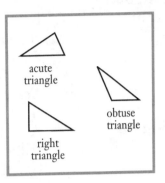

acute triangle

obtuse triangle

right triangle

acute triangle Each of the angles of an acute triangle is an acute angle (less than 90°).

obtuse triangle One of the angles of an obtuse triangle is an obtuse angle (greater than 90°).

right triangle One of the angles of a right triangle is a right angle (90°).

Related words triangular, triangulate

Did You Know?

The *tri-* in triangle means "*three.*" Words such as *tricycle, triathlon, tripod,* and *triplet* are related in meaning. A triangle is often used in construction because it is a very strong shape.

See also polygon.

triangular number

A triangular number is a number that can be shown in an array that looks like a triangle.

Examples
Arrays for the first five triangular numbers are shown.

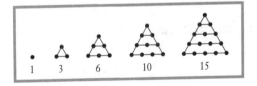

1   3   6   10   15

triangular prism

A triangular prism is a prism that has triangles as bases.

Example
This chocolate bar is in the shape of a triangular prism.

See also prism.

triangular pyramid

A triangular pyramid is a pyramid with a triangle-shaped base. If all faces are equilateral triangles, also called a regular tetrahedron. A triangular pyramid is also called a tetrahedron.

See also pyramid.

trillion

A trillion is equal to 1000 billions. In standard form, one trillion is written as 1,000,000,000,000. With an exponent, one trillion may be written as 1×10^{12} (or simply as 10^{12}).

See also decimal numeration system.

turn

A turn is the movement of a figure about a fixed point. Also called rotation.

See also slide; flip.

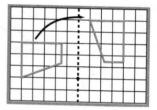

twenty-four-hour clock

A twenty-four-hour clock represents time beginning and ending at midnight. Some times on the twenty-four-hour clock and their twelve-hour-clock equivalents are

twenty-four-hour clock	twelve-hour clock
0100	1:00 AM
0400	4:00 AM
1300	1:00 PM
1545	3:45 PM

two-dimensional

Two-dimensional is a term used to describe plane figures.

See also geometric figure; one-dimensional; three-dimensional; zero-dimensional.

two-dimensional figure

A two-dimensional figure is a geometric figure that has area but no thickness. It lies entirely in one plane. Also called plane figure, plane shape, and two-dimensional shape.

See also plane figure.

unit price

Unit price is the cost per item or cost per unit of measure. Unit price can be expressed as a ratio. Also called cost per unit and unit cost.

Example—cost per item
Garth bought 2 erasers for $.50. How much did each eraser cost?
2:50 = 1:25
Each eraser cost $.25.
The unit price is $.25.

Example—cost per unit of measure
A 1-pound loaf of bread cost $1.60. What was the cost of the bread per 1-ounce serving? (1 pound = 16 ounces)
1.60:16 = .10:1
The unit price is $.10.

See also equal ratios.

unit fraction

A unit fraction is a fraction with a numerator of 1. A unit fraction can be expressed as the sum of two equal unit fractions.

Examples
$$\frac{1}{2} = \frac{1}{4} + \frac{1}{4}$$
$$\frac{1}{3} = \frac{1}{6} + \frac{1}{6}$$

A unit fraction can also be expressed as the sum of two different unit fractions.

Examples
$$\frac{1}{2} = \frac{1}{3} + \frac{1}{6}$$
$$\frac{1}{3} = \frac{1}{4} + \frac{1}{12}$$

Other fractions can also be named as the sum of unit fractions.

Examples
$$\frac{2}{3} = \frac{1}{2} + \frac{1}{6}$$
$$\frac{2}{7} = \frac{1}{4} + \frac{1}{28}$$

Did You Know?

An archaeological discovery called the Rhind papyrus shows that Egyptians used unit fractions in their mathematical work well over 3000 years ago. The Rhind papyrus is about 18 feet long and 1 foot wide. It is in the British Museum in London, England.

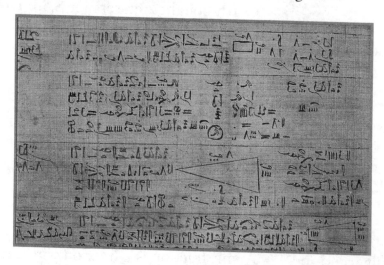

unlike fractions

Unlike fractions are fractions with different denominators.

Example

$\frac{1}{3}$ and $\frac{1}{2}$ are unlike fractions.

The denominator of $\frac{1}{3}$ is 3.

The denominator of $\frac{1}{2}$ is 2.

See also like fractions.

U.S. Customary System

The U.S. Customary System is the measurement system used most commonly in the United States. Also called customary measurement system, customary system, customary system of measurement, English measurement system, English system of measurement, and standard system of measurement.

See also customary system of measurement.

variable

A variable is a symbol that may be used to stand for an unknown number in an expression or equation. Usually a variable is written as a letter. Sometimes it is indicated by a ☐ or some other symbol.

Examples
$4 + \square = 9$
$A = l \times w$
$4n + 2 = 18$
$2x + y$

See also algebra.

Venn diagram

A Venn diagram is a diagram, usually made with circles, that shows relationships of sets.

This Venn diagram shows the sets of factors of 12 and 18. The factors that are the same for both numbers are included in the overlapping region. These members, or elements, are the same for the two sets.

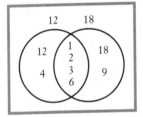

This Venn diagram shows that all squares are rectangles. Therefore, squares are a subset of rectangles.

It also shows that there are rectangles that are not squares.

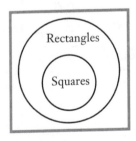

disjoint sets This Venn diagram shows that the sets of odd numbers and even numbers do not share any elements. (A number cannot be both odd and even.) Since the sets of odd numbers and even numbers do not share any elements, they are called disjoint sets.

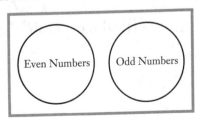

Did You Know?

Venn diagrams are named for John Venn, an English-man who lived from 1834 to 1923. Venn studied logic and developed diagrams as tools for logical thinking.

vertex

pl. **vertices** A vertex is a point at which two or more sides or edges of a geometric figure meet.

Examples
Point A is the vertex of this angle.

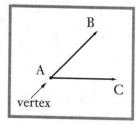

Points A, B, C, and D are the vertices of this rectangle.

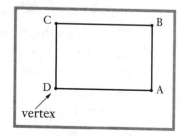

Points A, B, C, D, and E are the vertices of this square pyramid.

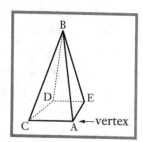

apex Point B is the vertex at the highest point in relation to the base of this pyramid. It is also known as the apex.

See also angle; apex.

vertical bar graph

In a vertical bar graph, the bars, or rectangles representing the data, run from the bottom to the top of the graph.

See also bar graph.

vertical axis

The vertical axis is the vertical number line in a rectangular coordinate system. Also called *y*-axis.

See also coordinate system; *y*-axis.

volume

The volume of a space figure is how much space it occupies. The volume of a container is how much it can hold. Volume is often measured in cubic units.

cubic unit Each edge of each square face of a cubic unit measures 1 unit.

Examples
The volume of this rectangular prism is 36 cubic units.

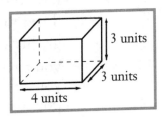

Below are some space figures and the formulas for finding their volume.

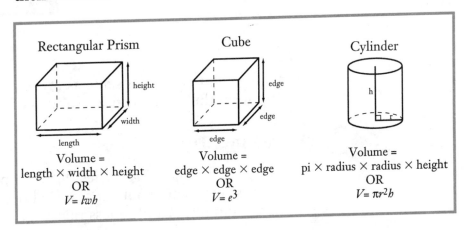

In the metric system of measurement, units of cubic measure include cm³, dm³, and m³. In the customary system, units of cubic measure include in.³, ft³, and yd³. When a container is used for holding liquids, its volume may be measured in units of capacity (cups, quarts, liters, and so on).

See also capacity; cubic unit.

weight

Weight is how heavy an object is. One way to find the weight of an object is to multiply the mass of the object by the gravity. (The abbreviation for *gravity*, g, is the same as the abbreviation for *gram*. Be careful not to confuse these two uses.)

Example
At sea level on Earth, gravity is 1, or 1 g. If you have a weight of 110 pounds, you would weigh 110×1, or 110 pounds at sea level on Earth.

The moon's gravity is $\frac{1}{6}$ of the gravity on Earth, or $\frac{1}{6}$ g. If you have a weight of 110 pounds, you would weigh about 18.3 pounds on the moon.

Although weight is not the same as mass, people often use them to mean the same outside the field of science.

 Did You Know?

You would weigh slightly less at the top of Mount Everest than you would at sea level because the gravity at the summit is a little less than 1 g.

Related word weigh

See also customary system of measurement; metric system of measurement.

whole numbers   Whole numbers are the numbers 0, 1, 2, 3, 4, ... They go on without end. They include all the counting numbers and 0.

A number line is a line (or line segment or ray) on which numbers are assigned points. It helps us see numbers in relation to each other.

On this number line showing whole numbers, we can see that 3 < 4 because 3 is closer to 0.

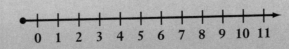

width   Width is the measure of an object from side to side.

See also length.

withdrawal   A withdrawal is money removed from a checking account or savings account.

Related word withdraw

See also deposit.

word form   The word form of a number is the number written as it is said in words. Also called word name for a number.

Examples
The word form for 14 is fourteen.
The word form for $\frac{1}{2}$ is one half.
The word form for 5.6 is five and six tenths.
(Notice that the decimal point is read as *and*.)
The word form for 2002 is two thousand two.
(Notice that the word *and* is not included in the word form.)
The word form for 1,000,000 is one million.

165

x- and y-axes

The *x*- and *y*-axes are the number lines used as references in a rectangular coordinate system.

See also coordinate system; *x*-axis; *y*-axis.

x-axis

The *x*-axis is the horizontal number line in a rectangular coordinate system. Also called horizontal axis.

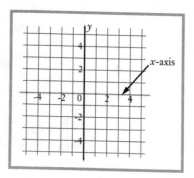

See also coordinate system.

x- and y-coordinates

The *x*- and *y*-coordinates are the two numbers in an ordered pair, used to identify a location on a map or in a rectangular coordinate system.

See also coordinate system; *x*-coordinate; *y*-coordinate.

x-coordinate

The *x*-coordinate indicates a distance along the *x*-axis, or horizontal axis, in a rectangular coordinate system. It is the first number in a set of two numbers called an ordered pair.

Example
In the ordered pair (3, 5),
3 is the *x*-coordinate.

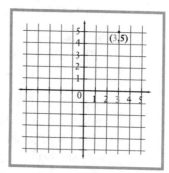

See also coordinate system; ordered pair; *y*-coordinate.

yard (yd)

A yard is a unit of length in the customary system of measurement.
1 yard = 3 feet or 36 inches

Did You Know?

In ancient times a yard may have been the length of the sash, or gird, worn around the king's waist. It is believed that King Henry I of England decreed a yard to be the distance from the tip of his nose to the end of his thumb.

See also customary system of measurement.

y-axis

The y-axis is the vertical number line in a rectangular coordinate system. Also called vertical axis.

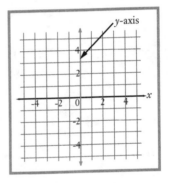

See also coordinate system.

y-coordinate

The y-coordinate indicates a distance along the y-axis, or vertical axis, in a coordinate system. It is the second number in a set of two numbers called an ordered pair.

Example
In the ordered pair (3, 5), 5 is the y-coordinate.

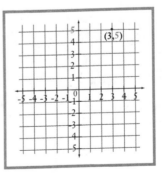

See also coordinate system; ordered pair; x-coordinate.

167

yd²

Read as *square yard*. A yd² is equal to the area enclosed by a square that measures 1 yard by 1 yard. Also written as square yard and sq yd.

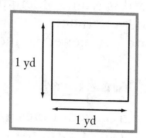

Did You Know?

The screens of some big-screen televisions have areas of about 1 square yard.

See also square unit.

yd³

Read as *cubic yard*. A yd³ is equal to the volume of a cube that measures 1 yard on each edge. Also written as cubic yard.

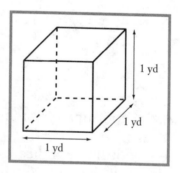

See also cubic unit.

zero

Zero is represented by the symbol 0. It has several meanings. Zero is the first whole number in the set of whole numbers. (In the set of integers, zero is neither positive nor negative.)

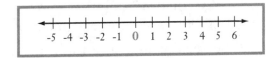

Zero is the number of members in the empty set.

Example
The number of basketball players taller than 9 feet is 0. There are no members in this set.

identity for addition Zero is the identity for addition. That is, the sum of 0 and any addend (number to be added) is equal to that addend.

Examples
$0 + 3 = 0$
$\frac{1}{4} + 0 = \frac{1}{4}$

placeholder In a number with more than one digit, 0 is the placeholder (holds the place) when there is no value for that place.

Examples
In the number 40, zero holds the ones place because there are no ones. In the number 2002, zero holds the hundreds and tens places because there are no hundreds or tens.

See also empty set; identity property for addition; zero property of multiplication.

zero-dimensional

A point is zero-dimensional because it does not occupy space. We cannot draw a picture of a point, since it has zero dimensions. We usually represent a point with a dot.

A
•

See also one-dimensional; three-dimensional; two-dimensional.

zero property of multiplication

The zero property of multiplication means that the product of any number and 0 is equal to 0. Also called zero product property.

Examples

5×0 (or 0×5) = 0

$\frac{3}{4} \times 0$ (or $0 \times \frac{3}{4}$) = 0

$^-2 \times 0$ (or $0 \times {}^-2$) = 0

$1{,}000{,}000 \times 0$ (or $0 \times 1{,}000{,}000$) = 0

The zero property of multiplication is written with symbols as

$a \times 0 = 0 \times a = 0.$

Z

Symbols

$+$	plus, as in $3 + 4$
$-$	minus, as in $6 - 2$
$\times$	times, as in 5×7
$\div$	divided by, as in $9 \div 3$
$=$	is equal to
$\neq$	is not equal to
$>$	is greater than
$<$	is less than
$\geq$	is greater than or equal to
$\leq$	is less than or equal to
$\$$	dollar sign
$\cent$	cent sign
$\%$	percent
π	pi (approximately 3.14)
$\circ$	degree
$^\circ\text{C}$	degree Celsius
$^\circ\text{F}$	degree Fahrenheit
$\ldots$	continuing without end
$1.\overline{3}$	repeating decimal $1.333\ldots$
$:$	is to, as in proportions, $a{:}b$ as $c{:}d$, which means $\frac{a}{b} = \frac{c}{d}$
$2{:}5$	ratio of 2 to 5
$^+4$	positive 4
$^-4$	negative 4
$\overleftrightarrow{AB}$	line AB
$\overline{AB}$	Line segment AB
$\overrightarrow{AB}$	ray AB
$\angle ABC$	angle ABC
$(3,4)$	ordered pair, 3, 4
(x,y)	coordinates of a point on a plane
$(\ )$	parentheses, shows order of operations, as in $(2 + 3) + 5 = 5 + 5 = 10$

Table of Measures
METRIC

Length

1 millimeter (mm)	=	0.001 meter (m)
1 centimeter (cm)	=	0.01 meter
1 decimeter (dm)	=	0.1 meter
1 dekameter (dam)	=	10 meters
1 hectometer (hm)	=	100 meters
1 kilometer	=	1000 meters

Mass/Weight

1 milligram (mg)	=	0.001 gram (g)
1 centigram (cg)	=	0.01 gram
1 decigram (dg)	=	0.1 gram
1 dekagram (dag)	=	10 grams
1 hectogram (hg)	=	100 grams
1 kilogram (kg)	=	1000 grams
1 metric ton (t)	=	1000 kilograms

Capacity

1 milliliter (mL)	=	0.001 liter (L)
1 centiliter (cL)	=	0.01 liter
1 deciliter (dL)	=	0.1 liter
1 dekaliter (daL)	=	10 liters
1 hectoliter (hL)	=	100 liters
1 kiloliter (kL)	=	1000 liters

In the metric system there is also a relationship between the units of capacity and the cubic units:

1 liter	=	1000 cubic centimeters (cm^3)
1 milliliter	=	1 cubic centimeter

Volume

1 cubic centimeter (cm^3)	=	1000 cubic millimeters (mm^3)
1 cubic decimeter (dm^3)	=	1000 cubic centimeters
1 cubic meter (m^3)	=	1,000,000 cubic centimeters

Area

1 square centimeter (cm^2)	=	100 square millimeters (mm^2)
1 square meter (m^2)	=	10,000 square centimeters
1 hectare (ha)	=	10,000 square meters
1 square kilometer (km^2)	=	1,000,000 square meters

Table of Measures
CUSTOMARY

Length

1 foot (ft)	=	12 inches (in.)
1 yard (yd)	=	36 inches
		3 feet
1 mile (mi)	=	5280 feet
		1760 yards
		320 rods
1 rod	=	16.5 feet
		5.5 yards

Mass/Weight

1 pound (lb)	=	16 ounces (oz)
1 ton (T)	=	2000 pounds

Capacity

1 cup (C)	=	8 fluid ounces (fl oz)
1 pint (pt)	=	2 cups
1 quart (qt)	=	2 pints
1 gallon (gal)	=	4 quarts
1 peck (pk)	=	8 quarts
1 bushel (bu)	=	4 pecks

Volume

1 cubic foot (ft^3)	=	1728 cubic inches ($in.^3$)
		7.5 gallons
		0.8 bushels
1 cubic yard (yd^3)	=	27 cubic feet
1 gallon	=	230.4 cubic inches

Area

1 square foot (ft^2)	=	144 square inches ($in.^2$)
1 square yard (yd^2)	=	9 square feet
1 acre	=	43,560 square feet
1 square mile (mi^2)	=	640 acres

Time

1 minute (min)	=	60 seconds (s)
1 hour (h)	=	60 minutes
1 day (d)	=	24 hours
1 week (wk)	=	7 days
1 year (yr)	=	12 months (mo)
		52 weeks
		365 days
1 decade	=	10 years
1 century (c)	=	100 years
1 millennium	=	1000 years

Photo Credits

All photographs by Silveer Burdett Ginn (SBG) unless otherwise noted.

References

Carroll, J.B. (ed.). (1956). *Language, thought and reality: Selected writings of Benjamin Lee Whorf.* New York: Technology Press of Massachusetts Institute of Technology, John Wiley & Sons.

Miller, D.L. (1993). Making the connection with language. *Arithmetic Teacher, 40*(6), 311–316.

National Council of Teachers of Mathematics. (1989). *Curriculum and evaluation standards of school mathematics.* Reston, VA: Author.

National Council of Teachers of Mathematics. (1991). *Professional standards for teaching mathematics.* Reston, VA: Author.

National Council of Teachers of Mathematics. (1995). *Assessment standards for school mathematics.* Reston, VA: Author.

Reutzel, D.R., & Cooter, R.B., Jr. (1996). *Teaching children to read: From basals to books* (2nd ed.). Englewood Cliffs, NJ: Prentice Hall.

Schell, V.J. (1982). *Learning partners: Reading and mathematics.* Reading Teacher, *35*(5), 544–548.